In the Moment

Conferring in the Elementary Math Classroom

Moment

Jen Munson

FOREWORD BY
Jo Boaler

HEINEMANN
Portsmouth, NH

Heinemann

361 Hanover Street

Portsmouth, NH 03801–3912

www.heinemann.com

Offices and agents throughout the world

Cataloging-in-Publication Data is on file with the Library of Congress.

ISBN: 978-0-325-09869-2

Editor: Katherine Bryant

Production Editor: Sonja S. Chapman

Interior Design: Shawn Girsberger

Typesetter: Shawn Girsberger

Cover Design: Suzanne Heiser

Cover Photo: Lauren Audet

Manufacturing: Steve Bernier

Printed in the United States of America on acid-free paper

2 3 4 5 6 CGB 24 23 22 21

March 2021 Printing

To Mary Trinkle, Faith Kwon, and Ruby Dellamano

Dedicated practitioners, fierce advocates, relentless learners

And to Viviana Espinosa, a principal who knows what matters

Contents

Video Clips

How to Access the Online Videos

To access the online resources for *In the Moment*, scan the QR code or go to http://hein.pub/IntheMoment-login to log in. If you do not already have an account with Heinemann you will need to create an account.

Register your product by entering the code: ITMOM

Once you have registered your product, it will appear in the list of My Online Resources.

COMPARING CONFERRING IN LITERACY AND MATH

Watch Mary compare her own practices of conferring in literacy and math.

WHAT IS A CONFERENCE?

In the following clip, Faith confers with two students who have been working on solving the following problem:

> **My mom has 20 packs of 10 Halloween pencils and 4 loose ones. How many Halloween pencils does she have? How do you know?**

As you watch this conference, consider:

- How do the teacher and students work together to make thinking visible?
- How does the teacher nudge student thinking forward?

In this conference, Faith elicits student thinking with a series of questions, supporting her students in making their thinking visible. Faith asks the students to show her the model they have created and prompts them to connect that model back to the task. These moves help the students realize that their model of two sticks of ten cubes doesn't match the story, and Faith nudges them to develop a new strategy to represent the mathematics and solve the problem.

THE ROLE OF RICH TASKS

In this clip, Faith reflects on the importance of choosing a rich and challenging task. Her second-grade students had been working on developing ideas about place value by counting collections of objects and forming groups of ten. On the previous day, the collections students counted ranged in size from 25 to about 90. Through conferring, Faith realized that this was no longer a rich task for these students because of what they had learned about tens and ones in two-digit numbers. Listen to how this task affected conferring and what task Faith plans to do next.

REFLECTIONS ON PROBING STUDENT THINKING

In this clip, Mary reflects on how learning moves to probe students' thinking helped her learn to confer in math in a way that was different from her conferring practice in literacy.

ELICITING STUDENT THINKING

Like all of conferring, eliciting looks different depending on the interaction. Watch the following clips of Mary and Faith eliciting their own students' thinking as they launch into conferring. As you watch, consider the following questions:

- What moves is the teacher using to make her students' thinking visible?
- How does the teacher follow up on students' thinking to surface more?
- What targeted moves do you notice?
- How and when does she probe for reasoning?
- How does the teacher engage all students?
- Which moves seem to be the most fruitful?

At the end of each clip, think about your interpretation of the students' thinking. Use the questions in the Forming an Interpretation section to reflect on the evidence surfaced through eliciting.

In this clip, Faith's second graders were continuing work on taking inventory of classroom materials by organizing them in packs or groups of ten and loose ones to build understanding of place value. These students were counting a bucket of foam geometric solids, when Faith began to elicit thinking about their counting.

In this clip, Faith's second graders were working to solve the problem:

My mom has 20 packs of 10 Halloween pencils and 4 loose ones. How many Halloween pencils does she have? How do you know?

Faith designed this task to push students beyond two-digit numbers while still thinking about tens and ones.

In this clip from Mary's fourth-grade class, students were asked to solve the following task:

The factory has an inventory of 381 small T-shirts. A customer bought 129 small T-shirts. How many small T-shirts are there now?

Mary approached a pair of students she had noticed from across the room were not collaborating. Notice how Mary uses different kinds of eliciting to uncover what was going on.

CONCEPTUAL UNDERSTANDING NUDGE

Faith's second graders were working on the following task:

My mom has 20 packs of 10 Halloween pencils and 4 loose ones. How many Halloween pencils does she have? How do you know?

In this conference, Faith's students were confused about the mathematical meaning of the task and wanted to represent the total number of pencils as 20 + 4. While the students had experience with thinking in tens and ones, they had never grappled with so many tens in a task. Faith nudges them on the meaning of 20 in this task and what a "pack of ten pencils" looks like, connecting the mathematics to the context of the story. Notice that Faith does not stay to guide them through the task but instead supports them in making meaning so they can get going.

DEVELOP A STRATEGY NUDGE

Mary wanted to push her student to think about the meaning of the traditional algorithm for subtraction, which they had learned in previous years, and to struggle with larger numbers when she offered her students some work produced by a fictional student the class named Jeffy. Jeffy had used this method to subtract 1,707 − 550, and he had gotten 1,257 as the result. The students are asked to figure out if Jeffy's work was correct and justify their decision. In the conference in this clip, Mary first elicits the students' thinking about what the task is and finds that the two partners disagree about whether Jeffy's work is accurate. Notice the moves that Mary uses to elicit and probe across the partnership and how she supports the students in connecting different strategies to make sense out of the subtraction. Note that Mary closes the conference when it is clear that the students have a plan, rather than walking through that plan with them step by step.

REPRESENTATION NUDGE

Faith's second graders were counting collections of objects by organizing them in groups of ten to deepen their understanding of place value. The students Faith confers with in this clip have organized a large collection of blocks into many groups of ten. Faith asks them to count these orally, and they confront what happens after 190. Faith nudges the students to figure out how they might represent the quantity with number names and numerals and how these two representations are related to place value.

COMMUNICATION NUDGE

This conference took place on the same day as the one shown in Clip 4.1, during which the second graders were asked to figure out how many pencils Faith's mom had when she bought 20 packs of ten and 4 loose ones. These students had first modeled this task as 2 sticks of ten cubes and 4 extra cubes, but then figured out how to model it as 20 sticks of ten cubes and 4 extra cubes. Faith nudges them to rehearse how to explain why they changed their mind to the whole class during the discussion.

RESPONDING TO THE BLANK STARE

5.1

Mary reflects on moments when she has received the blank stare, how she interprets this signal, and what she does next to get the conversation going again.

REFLECTIONS ON FOCUSING THE CLOSING DISCUSSION

6.1

Mary uses conferring data to inform how she orchestrates her closing discussions, which she calls the debrief. In this video clip, listen to how Mary reflects on her own process for making decisions about structuring the discussion based on what she learns about student thinking and strategies during the work time.

HOW CONFERRING CAN SHAPE THE NEXT LESSON

6.2

In this clip, Mary has just engaged her fourth graders in a lesson as part of a unit on subtraction in the context of a T-shirt factory in which the students keep track of the inventory of the factory as shirts are made and sold (Fosnot 2008). Mary had noticed at the beginning of this unit that her students used the traditional algorithm for subtraction but did not understand why it worked or what the numbers represented. Her goal was to support them in connecting the algorithm they already knew with other representations of subtraction to build meaning. The task she gave them on this day was to check whether or not the following solution for the inventory, made by a fictitious student, was correct, if the factory had 1,707 T-shirts and sold 550 of them.

$$\begin{array}{r} 1{,}707 \\ -\ 550 \\ \hline 1{,}257 \end{array}$$

Mary placed base ten blocks on the board to represent the 1,707 T-shirts so students could see the starting amount. They were then asked to work in partnerships to use the base ten blocks as evidence for whether or not the student's work was correct. During conferring, Mary encountered students who were deeply frustrated and confused. In the video, notice how Mary thinks through the data she gathered through conferring, what she learned in the closing discussion, and how she plans to use that data to shape her plans for the next day's lesson. Note also how Mary generates some theories about what may be causing her students' frustration and plans her work for the next day to help her test her ideas and learn more, developing her own pedagogical content knowledge (see page 108) as she does so.

6.3

In this clip, Faith reflects on what she learned about her second-grade students' understanding after a lesson in which they worked on counting classroom objects in groups of tens and loose ones and then recording their findings numerically. For instance, 7 packs of ten markers and 9 loose ones would be written as "79." The class had been doing this sort of counting for several days to support making connections between counting, place value, and written numbers. Faith describes some examples of what she observed while conferring and what she plans to try the next day to respond to ideas that emerged in two of her conferences. Notice that she uses her observations from this lesson to predict a misconception she might see the following day about how to write three-digit numbers. She then plans to use a recording sheet that will support students in thinking about the ways to write three-digit numbers to match what they stand for conceptually.

USING CONFERRING TO ANTICIPATE STUDENT THINKING

Faith reflects on what she noticed from her conferring during a task in which students were asked: If I have 20 packs of ten pencils and 4 loose ones, how many pencils do I have? The data she gathered across her class helps Faith map what makes the concept of place value challenging when students extend their thinking from two-digit numbers to three-digit numbers and the strategies that students could use to build their understanding of why this quantity is represented as 204 rather than 24. This is an example of using conferring to build pedagogical content knowledge around place value that can support Faith in her work with these students and future second graders.

HOW CONFERRING FITS IN

Mary reflects on how conferring holds her mathematics instruction together, and how she makes time to confer. Mary talks about the kinds of records she keeps and how she uses these day to day and across a unit of instruction.

PRACTICE: ELICITING, NOTICING, AND INTERPRETING

On this day Mary presented her students with the following task:

The factory has an inventory of 381 small T-shirts. A customer bought 129 small T-shirts. How many small T-shirts are there now?

She then showed them some work based on a common misconception in her class about how to model subtraction using base ten blocks. She showed how a fictitious student the class named Alex had represented 381 T-shirts with base ten blocks. The student had crossed out one hundred blocks and two tens rods. Then, seeing he didn't have enough ones left to cross out 9 ones, he added 9 ones instead. Mary asked the class to determine whether or not Alex's work was correct and come up with a justification for their answer. Watch the clip to see Mary elicit thinking from two students who partnered on this task.

The following two clips both took place the next day, when Mary again offered students work from a fictitious student, whom the class named Jeffy, and asked them to determine if and why it made sense. Jeffy had been solving a problem that involved starting with 1,707 T-shirts, then selling 550 of those shirts. When he subtracted using the traditional algorithm, he found that there were 1,257 T-shirts remaining. In this work Jeffy has made an error the students often make, simply subtracting the smaller digit from the larger one without attending to the meaning of what they are doing.

Mary and I conferred with two students on the carpet soon after the class started working on the task. Watch the clip to see the thinking elicited and how we navigate some blank stares.

 Mary conferred with this pair of students who quickly name that they are stuck. Watch the clip to see how Mary elicits thinking to better understand where these students are.

PRACTICE: MAKING DECISIONS TO NUDGE

 In this clip, Faith sits down with two students counting pattern blocks on the carpet. The class has learned to make groups of ten to make counting easier. Notice how Faith is observing surfacing student thinking as students work in this clip.

 The following two clips come from the same day, on which Faith presented students with the following task:

> **My mom bought a bunch of Halloween pencils. She bought 20 packs of 10 pencils and 4 loose ones. How many Halloween pencils did my mom buy?**

 Faith wanted them to grapple with numbers in the hundreds while still thinking with groups of ten. Watch these clips to see how Faith elicits students' thinking about this task and nudges that thinking forward when the partnerships have different ideas at the start of each conference.

Acknowledgments

This book would not have been possible without the many teachers and children from whom I have learned over my years as a coach and, now, as a researcher. I learned what children's mathematical thinking can look like and what patient, curious, and daring teaching could sound like alongside many professionals in classrooms across the country. I am forever grateful for the audacity of Mary Trinkle, Faith Kwon, and Ruby Dellamano—who would have appeared in this book if she had not become a teacher on special assignment in the year of filming. Many thanks to Viviana Espinosa, the principal of Costaño Elementary School in East Palo Alto. This project would have been deeply impoverished without your leadership. I have learned every year from my long-term partnership with Lyon Elementary School in Magnolia, Texas; thanks especially to Misty Anderson, Tammy Haley, Cindy Hill, Barbara McClanahan, Jenny Taylor, Chelsea Vasquez, and Jenny Maxwell. Thanks to Rebecca Munson, who is utterly supportive, asks tough questions, and never lets me get away with a simple answer. My thinking about conferring in math as a pedagogy that others might learn began with coaching work in collaboration with the teachers, coaches, and leaders at Capital City Public Charter School, the schools of the DC Collaborative for Change, and Teachers Institute.

Seeing conferring in action with children makes all the difference. My gratitude to the Ravenswood City School District for permission to film, and to the Costaño families who trusted me and my intent. Although I have filmed for research studies before, I had no idea what it takes to get great video (and audio) until I watched professionals in action. I could not believe my luck to work with Sherry Day, Michael Grover, Dennis Doyle, Alan Chow, Lauren Audet, and the incredible Katherine Bryant. I am deeply indebted to Katherine, who shepherded this project from a presentation at the National Council of Teachers of Mathematics' Annual Meeting into the book in your hands. As an editor, Katherine provided the gentle, knowledgeable, and incisive feedback every writer needs. My thinking is clearer, my ideas are sharper, and this book is far, far better because of her deft hand.

The thinking and research on which this book is based is the direct result of years of serious conversations about mathematics, discourse, pedagogy, teacher learning, identity, agency, and authority with Jo Boaler, Jenny Langer-Osuna, and Maren Aukerman. Jo and Jenny have both helped me build my own personal bridge between research and practice and consider how to live and think in both worlds. I have benefited from the feedback and critical eyes of Maren's informal research group: Soyoung Park, Harper Keenan, Lisel Murdock-Perriera, Paolo Martin, Ziva Hassenfeld, Suki Jones Mozenter, and Liam Aiello. Thanks to Ramón Antonio Martínez for analytic advice, professional guidance, and friendship, and to Deborah Ball for early advice about analyzing conferring data as a researcher with an eye on practitioners.

At Stanford, I have been lucky to be part of a community of critical and analytical educators who have challenged me to think more deeply and made my work stronger at every turn. Endless thanks to my writing group Sarah McGrew and Mary Hauser without whom I would not have found the writer hidden inside of me. I am fortunate to collaborate with and count as a friend Cathy Williams, who inspires me to ask mathematical questions and gives our work energy. And to the Math Education Research Group, past and present, who have fed, shaped, and polished my ideas until they were ready to enter the world, I cannot express enough gratitude: Erin Baldinger, Sarah Kate Selling, Jenny Ruef, Holly Pope, Kathy Liu Sun, Anthony Villa III, Emma Gargroetzi, Melissa Kemmerle, Cathy Humphreys, and Rosa Chavez. I want to especially thank Charmaine Mangram, who looked at my ideas when I first arrived and told me I had something to say.

I would not find myself in the position to write anything if it hadn't been for my coaching colleague, Tamyka Morant. Many thanks for your scholarship, partnership, friendship, and the encouragement to go for it. When my career took an unexpected turn, Tamyka, along with Karen Dresden and Amy Wendel, supported me in heading off to Stanford, even though it meant leaving D.C. and my regular collaborations with them and their schools.

Finally, I am grateful for the support of my family. My partner, Matt, and our kids, Lola and Ruby, managed to be genuinely happy for me to have the opportunity to write this book, even when we all knew it meant fewer hours together. Many thanks also to my extended family who never fail to be my cheerleaders: Bobbi and Arnold, for becoming my parents when I needed some; Rebecca, for being proud of me and a professional colleague even at Thanksgiving; and Carolyn, for unfailing love and perseverance. You all model for me what it means to be a family.

Foreword by Jo Boaler

The Most Important Moments

This wonderful book focuses upon one of the most important moments in teaching—the time when teachers and students talk together and there is an opportunity for students to learn. Much of the literature and research on teaching presents the act of teaching in more general terms—focusing upon curriculum, student grouping, content knowledge, decisions that can be made before any teaching happens. But so much of what is important in classrooms happens inside classroom interactions between teachers and students. This book is all about those moments, and because of this it is a rare treasure.

In my work over recent years working with neuroscientists, exploring the ways our brain functioning can improve mathematics learning, I have learned about the importance of times of struggle for learning and brain development. Anders Ericsson is a psychologist who has studied expertise for decades, considering what it looks like and how it is developed. Ericsson coined the term "deliberate practice" to describe the most effective type of practice. At the heart of deliberate practice is the opportunity for learners to learn from a more knowledgeable other and for that person to coach the learner, giving feedback on their learning. Ericsson talks about the importance of learners being at the edge of their understanding, making mistakes, correcting them, and making more.

The highly effective mistakes-based practice Ericsson discusses has also been identified by Daniel Coyle in his book *The Talent Code*. Coyle set out to study people in all sorts of fields who had the most extreme talent. He found that what was common to all of them was not a genetic advantage but engagement in a particular type of practice. Coyle describes the practice, similar to Ericsson, as people pushing at the edge of their understanding, making mistakes, correcting them, and continuing on. The coaching that both authors focus on, giving timely feedback to learners, happens in the moments of teaching that are the focus of this book—what Jen has called conferring: "A math conference uncovers and advances student thinking . . . it is a chance to learn together in the moment." The work of Ericsson and Coyle suggest that these moments are some of the most important opportunities in teaching.

When Jen started her doctoral study of conferring interactions I was thrilled as I knew these were an understudied yet critically important time in teaching. We know that it is productive for students to struggle and to work on difficult work that will push them at "the edge of their understanding" but the culture of teaching in the United States. has meant that teachers are more likely to jump in and "save" students when they struggle. This "saving," which often means breaking work down into small manageable chunks, may feel good to students but usually empties tasks of their cognitive demand and robs the interaction of the opportunity for deep learning. But if teachers should not help students by breaking down questions into manageable sections, what do they do instead? How should teachers handle those moments of struggle? Teachers know that these are important times, when students' self-esteem and confidence is often on the line. This book provides teachers with the important knowledge they need in these critical moments, with lots of rich and detailed examples of conversations to have, questions to ask students, and areas to focus upon.

One of Jen's contributions to the field of educational work in this area is her identification of a process she calls conferring. In the process of conferring teachers elicit student thinking to make it visible and "nudge" their thinking forward. This is that moment of coaching that is highlighted in the work of Andersson and Coyle, and the pages ahead zoom in on this important process. In the pages that follow teachers will learn what to do in those moments, ways to probe student thinking, ways to interpret student ideas and, importantly, ways to push understanding to a higher place. The examples Jen draws from do not come from educational theory; they come from the actual teaching practice of the teachers she worked with and studied for over a year. This is why the pages that follow are so readable, so fascinating, and so important.

It is my firm belief that to improve students' mathematical understanding in the United States, a clear area of need, we need to focus on and invest in teaching and teachers. In the last decade vast amounts of money and time have been spent on curriculum design and on standards. Both of these are important, but we have neglected the important interactions that happen inside classrooms where learning happens. In this valuable book Jen provides us with a tool to advance teaching and to equip teachers with the knowledge and ideas to try inside these moments. I expect that the pages that follow will be a guide that teachers will treasure for many years to come.

Introduction

Not so long ago, I found myself huddled around a table with three fourth graders who had been thinking about the following problem: How much is the shaded part of this rectangle?

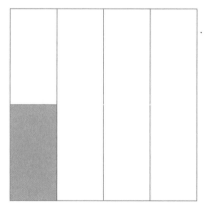

The group had decided that this blue part was $\frac{1}{2}\frac{1}{4}$. I thought this was marvelous. What inventive thinking they had engaged in to use what they knew about fractions—that partitioning a shape into two equal parts makes halves and partitioning a shape into four equal parts makes fourths—to name this unknown region. They told me all about how they had come to this idea and why it made sense to call this space "half fourth." And in so many ways they are right—it does make sense. Later when these students think about multiplying fractions, the idea that this portion could be thought of as $\frac{1}{2}$ of $\frac{1}{4}$ will help them think about why $\frac{1}{2} \times \frac{1}{4}$ is $\frac{1}{8}$.

But coming back to that day, in that moment, after I had learned about the reasoning that had generated their unconventional solution, what could I say to them? How could I respond, so that I supported their sense making *and* move them toward seeing eighths? These questions, of how to respond productively in the moment to the thinking students are developing right now, have driven my work for almost twenty years and are at the heart of this book.

When I first started teaching, I got very lucky. I arrived in my new district just north of Seattle at the same time as a new curriculum adoption. The tasks were rich; they asked students to stretch and invent. I was told to try these out, to talk to kids while they worked together, and to not say too much. As a new teacher looking for guidance, I soaked up this advice and all the time I had with my colleagues to talk about math teaching. We all had a hard time learning how much to say to students, what questions to ask, when to let them struggle, and when and how to step in. When my kids were working, I walked around the room, listening in and stopping to talk with them about their thinking. I quickly learned that although I loved talking with my colleagues at our monthly meetings, I spent much more time talking with children every day. If I was going to learn how to support them, I was going to learn it from them. The children in my classes taught me what to say and how to listen, and it changed everything for me.

Since those first few years, I have taught in schools in Chicago and Washington, D.C., and worked with teachers and their students in schools across the country. And in every place, I have learned from teachers and children as they talk to one another about mathematics. These conversations—just a few minutes long—in the midst of learning are jewel boxes of instruction. They contain everything teaching should offer: the opportunity for students to name and grow their own ideas, productive struggle, formative assessment, and a differentiated response. When these conversations went well, I could see learning happening, and this fed my curiosity. Why do some of these conversations feel so productive and powerful? Why do some feel like slogging? What do I do when I can't seem to understand what the children are thinking, and they don't understand me? How do I know what each child understands?

I wanted to understand conferring in mathematics because I believe these interactions have the potential to provide immediate, differentiated instruction to students right when they need it. Conferring means that you don't wait until tomorrow, or Friday, or the end of the unit to know what kids need and provide it. You can be there with them in the tiny moments when their thinking is growing—or floundering—and provide the next little nudge they need to grow even more. Now, as a researcher, I focus on understanding how conferring interactions work and how teachers learn to respond to student thinking in the moment. This book is based on my experience as a teacher and math coach and on the results of studies I have conducted in elementary classrooms.

Conferring Here, There, and Everywhere

You may be familiar with the idea of conferring in reading and writing instruction (c.f., Anderson 2000; Calkins 1986, 2001). In all disciplines, conferring is the practice of talking with students as they engage in meaningful work with the purpose of uncovering their thinking and supporting learning in the moment. Uncovering student thinking looks similar regardless of the age or subject matter—we ask students questions, we watch what they do and say, and we read what they are writing and drawing (Teaching Works 2014).

But how we support students' learning in the moment varies depending on whether we teach writing, science, reading, social studies, or math, because each involves somewhat different ways of thinking, solving, explaining, justifying, gathering evidence, interpreting, representing, and dealing with ambiguity. In thinking about conferring in mathematics, I consider the disciplinary practices of mathematics, such as those described in the Standards for Mathematical Practice (Common Core State Standards Initiative 2010). Students collaborate to invent, try, refine, represent, and justify ways of tackling challenging mathematical tasks. Conferring in math should respond to and support students in this kind of work.

Math, for instance, is a social act: students work together, in pairs and small groups, to solve problems and build understanding. So, conferring in math involves the teacher stepping into this social mathematical space to support the learning, communication, and participation of all partners. In math, children are solving problems, and the journey to a solution is more valuable than the destination. So, conferring in math must position the teacher alongside students on their pathway, rather than as the beacon at the end of the trail guiding them home. Conferring in math asks, "Where are you?" and "Where could you go next?" rather than "Where should you be?" or "What would *I* do next?"

The Goals of Conferring in Mathematics

Conferring in mathematics has several goals, including providing differentiated instruction, promoting equity and inclusion, supporting norms for discourse and mathematical practices, and developing deep conceptual understanding. Let's take a brief look these goals and the role conferring with students as they work together to solve problems can play in them.

■ **DIFFERENTIATING INSTRUCTION.** We know that classrooms are not one-size-fits-all places, and to meet the needs of all students, teachers must provide differentiated instruction. This involves assessing what each student needs, what they are working on conceptually, and supporting their growth from where they are. This can be a challenging goal when viewed through the lens of whole-class instruction, but conferring with students creates multiple opportunities in every lesson to hear what individual students are thinking and provide them with the nudge they need to grow in the moment.

■ **PROMOTING EQUITY AND INCLUSION.** Not all students feel that they belong in math, or even in school. They may feel that their voices are not valued, that they do not have the authority to fully participate, or that their experiences in the past have not prepared them to feel competent and secure enough to take intellectual risks. Bringing every student into mathematics, so that they feel safe enough to make mistakes, certain that their ideas will be treated as worthy of consideration, and positioned to be the authority on what makes sense, must be a central goal of math teaching. Conferring gives teachers the opportunity to assess who is being excluded and to make deliberate moves to structure more equitable discourse between students. Teachers can, during each brief conversation, model how important each student's thinking is and how we talk and listen to one another.

■ **SUPPORTING NORMS FOR DISCOURSE AND MATHEMATICAL PRACTICES.** Perhaps the most important mathematical outcome of our teaching is helping students understand how to do math, and what *doing math* really is. As students engage in mathematical work, they are learning to persevere, make sense, explain, justify, model, convince, revise, generalize, and wonder, among many other practices. They can carry these practices with them for a lifetime of mathematical thinking. Conferring is a space to engage in these practices with students, scaffolding what participating in each one sounds and looks like, and making them explicit and learnable. Each time you confer with a group of students you have the chance to point out just where a particular practice would be useful and support students in trying it out.

■ **DEVELOPING DEEP CONCEPTUAL UNDERSTANDING.** Math is about thinking and understanding, rather than answers and procedures. Math makes sense, and students need opportunities to make sense of math. Given rich mathematical tasks, appropriate tools, and the chance to talk and think together, students will do just that. Conferring steps into students' ongoing and evolving thinking and keeps them in charge of making sense, while helping them think through what they need and what they might try.

These goals are reflected in the National Council of Teachers of Mathematics' *Principles to Actions* (2014) and the decades of research that document is based on. Conferring is just one way to strive toward achieving a classroom in which students make sense of math equitably, actively, daily. Although conferring serves lofty goals, it is also teaching at its most intimate—just you and a couple of children in this one moment. What you might say is specific to these children, in this moment. In this book, we'll focus on how the structure of conferring can support understanding children's thinking and then finding a specific, useful response that makes a difference in how they think, the way they engage in math, or the way they interact with one another.

How to Use This Book

This book is structured to support you to first build a vision of what conferring in math can look like and then unpack these interactions into parts that you can learn. We'll consider what else is happening in math and how conferring fits into your math teaching. And we'll dive into the challenges you may face as you learn with children.

■ **CHAPTER 1: What Is a Math Conference?** In this chapter we'll look at examples of what a conference does and does not look like. We'll look at the architecture of conferring, including what teachers say and what they think as the interaction unfolds.

■ **CHAPTER 2: Setting the Stage: Creating the Conditions for Conferring.** Conferring is just part of the teaching you do in mathematics. In this chapter we'll examine how rich tasks and norms for mathematical work support conferring and how conferring fits into the math lesson.

- **CHAPTER 3: Eliciting and Interpreting: What Are They Doing?** In this chapter we take a deep look at the first part of conferring, in which teachers and students work together to make students' thinking, work, and struggle visible. We'll examine the importance of the stance you bring with you to each conversation. We'll look at the moves teachers can use and how to interpret what students offer in response.

- **CHAPTER 4: Nudging: Growing Student Thinking in the Moment.** In this chapter we look at how you can decide what students might need next to advance their thinking and how to act on that decision. The chapter describes five types of nudges students may need and a set of moves you can use to nudge student thinking.

- **CHAPTER 5: Common Challenges.** This chapter examines three of the most common challenges teachers face when conferring and three possible responses to these challenges you can use in the moment to get conferring back on track.

- **CHAPTER 6: Using Conferring as Formative Assessment.** Conferring is both a way to advance student thinking and rich data you can use to inform instruction. In this chapter, we'll look at four ways you can use the data you gather to plan for instruction and ways to keep records.

- **CHAPTER 7: Learning to Confer.** In this chapter we'll consider activities you can engage in—on your own, with a learning partner, or in a group—that can support you in learning to confer. The chapter closes with a small video bank of examples of eliciting and nudging that you can analyze and discuss.

At the end of each chapter you'll find a short set of frequently asked questions related to the content of that chapter and a set of reflection questions designed to support you in thinking about your practice, talking with colleagues, and setting goals.

Along the way, you'll find links to video embedded in each chapter. These videos were taken at Costaño Elementary School in northern California. Costaño is a Title I school that serves a predominately Latinx and Pacific Islander neighborhood, in which nearly all families qualify for free and reduced lunch. Approximately 60 percent of students are classified by the state as English language learners. Within this school, you'll meet two teachers who have worked to develop their conferring practice in mathematics.

FAITH KWON is a second-grade teacher who has been teaching for four years. She taught first grade for the last three years, and this is her first year in second grade. She serves as a site teacher leader and district literacy lead. Faith confers in math because "I'm able to continue to grow the meaningful bonds I have with students, formatively assess their needs by listening in on their thinking, then leverage their strengths through strategic nudges."

MARY TRINKLE is a fourth-grade teacher who has been teaching for six years and is a committed learner. She is a site lead teacher and has previously supported professional development efforts in mathematics in her building and district. Mary confers in math for many reasons: "It's interesting to hear all the different ways the students grapple with concepts. I am able to see where my students' learning is, I am able to support their thinking and learning with a nudge, and what I notice supports how I debrief at the end of work time."

Throughout the book, you'll see videos of Mary and Faith conferring with their own students

COMPARING CONFERRING IN LITERACY AND MATH

Watch Mary compare her own practices of conferring in literacy and math.

during math and interviews of their reflections on conferring. These videos are intended to show how conferring can and does unfold with real children, in all its complexity, and how teachers think through the issues and questions that emerge.

How to Access the Online Videos

To access the online resources for *In the Moment*, scan the QR code or go to http://hein.pub/IntheMoment-login to log in. If you do not already have an account with Heinemann you will need to create an account.

Register your product by entering the code: ITMOM

Once you have registered your product, it will appear in the list of My Online Resources.

1

What Is a Math Conference?

onica's and Sofia's fourth graders are buzzing, huddled together in twos and threes around tables, holding rulers and yardsticks against the wall, and darting in and out of the hallway to examine artifacts their teachers have placed there—index cards posted at the heights of real people. There are athletes on the wall, singers, and the school principal, and each height is labeled either in feet and inches, as we usually name a person's height, or in inches only, as your doctor might measure you at a checkup. The challenge Monica and Sofia have coplanned today for their fourth-grade classes is to work in groups to develop a strategy for moving between the two ways of expressing height. How do we change feet and inches to inches only? How do we move from inches to feet? The teachers'

emphasis is on the idea of developing a strategy, because their students can use the strategy across multiple situations, and the process of developing a strategy for this problem will support them when they encounter other unfamiliar problems, say with weight or volume. As the students work in the two adjacent classrooms, the teachers circulate. Each dips into conversation with pairs and trios to find out what the students are doing and find ways to support their thinking.

Midway through the kids' work time, Monica pulls up next to two partners who have been working on converting two heights—85 inches and 77 inches—into feet and inches. Here's how their interaction unfolds:

MONICA: What did you two do over here?

WYATT: We did the multiples of 12—.

LIANI (*overlapping*): We did 12.

WYATT: We did the multiples of 12, and then for 85 inches we got the closest is 84.

LIANI: Yeah, 84.

WYATT: And then, it was 7, so it's 7 foot out of, because the 12 inches is 1 foot—.

LIANI (*overlapping*): Because the 12—.

MONICA: Mm-hmm.

LIANI: So we did the multiples of 12 and then we, that's 7—.

MONICA: Mm-hmm.

LIANI: So then 7, and then we added just 84 + 1 equals 85.

MONICA: Mm-hmm.

LIANI: So we just add 1 inch, so it's, it's 7 foot and 1 inch.

MONICA: Good job. That's really good. So you counted yours in multiples of 12.

LIANI: Mm-hmm.

WYATT: Just like we did the same thing for this one. And we did, and we just added the 5 inches to that, and added, and had 72 + 5, 77 inches.

MONICA: Good job. Really good job.

Wyatt and Liani have revealed a lot of their thinking. They have developed a strategy that involves a lot of understanding of the task, of the relationship between inches and feet, and how multiples might be useful in this relationship. When Monica closes the interaction by saying that the students have done a good job, she's right—they have done some very interesting sense-making. And Monica has created a space for that thinking. Students don't offer the kinds of details Wyatt and Liani do—and certainly with so little prompting— unless they believe their reasoning is expected and valued. At the end of this conversation, Wyatt and Liani know they have done their job and done it well. But where do Wyatt and Liani go now? What has grown or changed about their thinking through this interaction? Are they poised to build on their work?

At about the same time next door, Sofia approaches Vanessa and Orlando. The two are hovering over the same paper, where they had been developing a method for converting 6 feet 5 inches into inches only, the opposite of what Wyatt and Liani were trying.

SOFIA: OK. So what kind of ideas have you come up with?

VANESSA: First 'cause there's 12 inches in each foot, I would do, like, 6 feet times 12 inches in each foot would give you 72 inches. Then you add the leftover 5 inches and get 77 inches total.

SOFIA: OK. So, what made you think that? How did you know to do that?

VANESSA: I was thinking of equal groups of like 12 inches, equal groups of 12.

SOFIA: OK . . . and how come you just added 5 in there at the end?

VANESSA: Because it's 6 feet, 5 inches. 5 inches is not a foot, so you have to add that in. It's left over from the 6 feet.

SOFIA: OK. And how would you go and explain that to somebody else? Is there a way to draw a picture or explain it in a way for somebody else to understand?

ORLANDO: I guess we could draw a picture . . . somehow. Like we, instead of—.

VANESSA (*interrupting*): Oh, yeah, 6 circles with 12 inches in them . . . plus the remainder of 5.

ORLANDO (*overlapping*): Yeah, yeah, that's what I was thinking! Yeah, you could do that to explain it!

SOFIA: Very interesting. I'm going to come back and check that out.

These students also reveal a lot of their thinking, and they, too, have done a good job. But Sofia does not stop with uncovering Vanessa and Orlando's thinking. When Sofia asks, "Is there a way to draw a picture or explain it?" she pushes their thinking forward. We can imagine what Vanessa and Orlando will do next because of this conversation. This is a conference.

In this chapter, we will build a vision of what math conferences look and sound like by looking closely at some examples from real classrooms. How does a conference work? What do teachers think about? What do they say? We will then look at a general process for conferring that addresses these questions and helps us think about how teachers take an interaction and turn it into a conference. Let's start with Sofia.

What Is a Math Conference?

A math conference uncovers and advances student thinking. Both Monica and Sofia uncover student thinking, but only Sofia advances it. This is a crucial distinction. A conference is not simply a venue for students to report on their thinking. A conference is a shared opportunity for teachers and students to learn together in the moment. Let's examine how Sofia, Vanessa, and Orlando accomplish this by revisiting their conference.

Eliciting Information and Probing for More

Sofia starts her interaction with Vanessa and Orlando very much like Monica. She opens with a general question to *elicit* student thinking. Although it can often take several questions to elicit a full explanation from students, in this case Vanessa readily offers quite a lot of information about the process she and Orlando had developed to convert 6 feet 5 inches into inches only.

SOFIA: OK. So what kind of ideas have you come up with?

VANESSA: First 'cause there's 12 inches in each foot, I would do, like, 6 feet times 12 inches in each foot would give you 72 inches. Then you add the leftover 5 inches and get 77 inches total.

From this we can see that Vanessa is thinking about the number of inches in each foot and using multiplication to convert the feet into inches. Then she attends to the "leftover 5 inches" by adding them on. This is a generalizable process that makes mathematical sense. A teacher could be satisfied that these students understand and have achieved the content objective for the day. But in this case Sofia wants to know more about the reasoning that supports this process and how the pair arrived at this idea. Note that Monica did not do this in her conversation. Instead she closed the interaction with praise, and in doing so she missed the opportunity to deepen and extend student thinking the way Sofia does next.

SOFIA: OK. So, what made you think that? How did you know to do that?

VANESSA: I was thinking of equal groups of like 12 inches, equal groups of 12.

SOFIA: OK, and how come you just added 5 in there at the end?

VANESSA: Because it's 6 feet, 5 inches. 5 inches is not a foot, so you have to add that in. It's left over from the 6 feet.

What Sofia does here is *probing reasoning*. Probing gets beyond *what* students did and focuses attention on *why* they did it and *why* it makes sense. Vanessa had already given some reasoning, telling Sofia that there were 12 inches in each foot, but in this part of the interaction she expands on why multiplying and then adding makes sense. Multiplication makes sense because each foot is an equal group of 12 inches. But "5 inches is not a foot" and so cannot make another equal group; it must be added on at the end. By probing reasoning, Sofia has given Vanessa an opportunity to make additional connections in her justification. Sofia has also made more of Vanessa and Orlando's thinking visible so that as a teacher she can assess how the pair is making sense of the mathematics.

Not all conferences include probing reasoning. Whether or not teachers choose to probe depends on what students have already shared. In this case, Vanessa shared a lot about the process they had already developed and so Sofia decided to uncover the reasoning that was driving her process. In Chapter 3, we'll see instances where teachers made different choices based on what they were seeing in students' thinking and work, like choosing to focus on the collaboration between students or how to interpret the task.

Pushing Forward: What Makes a Conference a Conference?

In these first few moments of the interaction, Sofia and her students have reached a shared understanding of the work in progress. But a look at their written work shows that little of the thinking they've shared is recorded. Now, instead of closing the interaction, the teacher uses what she has learned to push their thinking forward, beyond what they have already done. It is in the following moment that the interaction truly becomes a conference.

SOFIA: OK. And how would you go and explain that to somebody else? Is there a way to draw a picture or explain it in a way for somebody else to understand?

ORLANDO: I guess we could draw a picture . . . somehow. Like we, instead of—.

VANESSA *(interrupting):* Oh, yeah, 6 circles with 12 inches in them . . . plus the remainder of 5.

ORLANDO *(overlapping):* Yeah, yeah, that's what I was thinking! Yeah, you could do that to explain it!

SOFIA: Very interesting. I'm going to come back and check that out.

Sofia pushes—she *nudges*—the students here to think about how they could extend their work. She actually offers them two ideas: explaining to others or representing their strategy using a drawing. In this case, Orlando takes up the idea of drawing a picture, though at first he isn't certain how. He and Vanessa work together—interrupting and talking on top of each other in their excitement—to craft a plan for how to turn their strategy into a picture. It's important to note that Sofia doesn't tell them *what* picture to draw. She simply suggests with her question that creating a picture could make their process clearer to someone else. The students figure out what kind of picture could accurately represent their thinking. Sofia makes encouraging sounds, and then finally closes this conference, not with

In the following clip, Faith confers with two students who have been working on solving the following problem:

My mom has 20 packs of 10 Halloween pencils and 4 loose ones. How many Halloween pencils does she have? How do you know?

As you watch this conference, consider:

- How do the teacher and students work together to make thinking visible?
- How does the teacher nudge student thinking forward?

In this conference, Faith elicits student thinking with a series of questions, supporting her students in making their thinking visible. Faith asks the students to show her the model they have created and prompts them to connect that model back to the task. These moves help the students realize that their model of 2 sticks of 10 cubes doesn't match the story, and Faith nudges them to develop a new strategy to represent the mathematics and solve the problem.

praise, but with the promise to return and see how their representation comes to life. In walking away, Sofia has a solid sense of what these two students understand and what they are going to do next, and all of it came from students' own thinking.

Sofia's nudge, which leads Vanessa and Orlando to represent their strategy with a picture, is what separates this interaction from Monica's. In a math conference, teachers always do two critical things:

1. Elicit student thinking to make it visible.
2. Nudge student thinking or work forward.

Certainly, every conference is different, but these two elements are always present. In Monica's interaction with Wyatt and Liani, she focused solely on eliciting student thinking. She and her students worked together to make their thinking visible, which itself has value as an opportunity to articulate and explain. At the close of the interaction, however, the students' work has not been advanced, extended, or challenged. The focus of much of this book is learning how to elicit and nudge student thinking in the many ways students need from us when we confer.

These examples show us what a conference can look like, but there is quite a lot going on under the surface. Let's take a deeper look at the process of conferring and make the invisible parts public.

The Conferring Process

Learning how to confer is difficult because, even though we ask students to make their thinking visible, teachers' thinking often remains invisible. If we listened in on a conference, we could hear the teacher eliciting student thinking and nudging that thinking forward. But what is that teacher thinking about? When a teacher approaches students at work, she immediately engages in a particular kind of thinking called *noticing* (Jacobs, Lamb, and Philipp 2010). Noticing involves *attending* to things that seem important, *interpreting* those details to give them meaning, and then *deciding how to respond*. In the following sections, we'll examine how thinking is connected to the conversation we can hear in each stage.

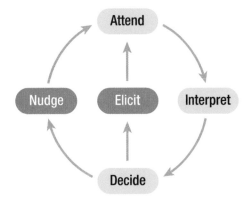

The conferring process, beginning with attending. The lighter cells are ways teachers think while conferring, and the darker green cells are actions teachers take.

Building an Interpretation of Student Thinking

Conferring is built on learning what students are doing and how they are thinking. In the first stage of a math conference, the teacher looks, listens, and asks with the goal of building an interpretation of student thinking at this moment. Throughout this stage the teacher is pondering a series of guiding questions:

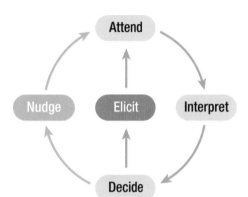

- What do students understand or misunderstand?
- What are students trying?
- What are they struggling with and why?
- Where are they in their process?

Attend

In the first moments of a math conference, the teacher does a number of things to begin to gather information. She very likely looks at the physical work students are doing, including written work and manipulatives and how they are moving or gesturing. She listens to what they are saying to each other or muttering to themselves. The teacher begins to pick out details that may be important to helping her understand what the students are doing and how they are making sense. She might attend to the particular way a child is counting cubes, the numbers the child has written on his paper, or who seems to be making decisions in the partnership. This is *attending*.

Elicit

Often, when we as teachers come in midstream, simply watching and listening doesn't provide enough clues for us to fully understand what has come before. So, we decide to ask questions. We elicit student thinking to give us more details to attend to. Most often teachers will start eliciting with a generic question that invites student to share their thinking, as both Monica and Sofia did. These moves can be as simple as "What are you trying?" or "What are you working on?" or "Tell me what you're doing?" These kinds of questions, when asked routinely, set the expectation that students explain their thinking and their process.

Even with this expectation, students often struggle to put words to their thinking. When students are struggling to articulate or offer partial explanations, teachers must ask follow-up elicitation questions to get a fuller picture of what students are working on. For instance, the teacher might ask, "You said you added 15 and 7. Where did those numbers come from?" or "What did you do next?" Teachers might also probe student thinking at this stage to learn how much children understand about why their process works, as Sofia did.

Interpret

The teacher begins to assemble all of these details from looking, listening, and asking into an interpretation of student thinking. A solid interpretation is grounded in evidence, in all the details the teacher has collected. The teacher might test her interpretation with some questions or by revoicing what she thinks she's heard from the student. In this way the teacher weaves between attending to, eliciting, and interpreting student thinking until she feels she has an interpretation that makes sense with all the evidence. An interpretation typically includes what the children understand and do not yet understand, what the children are trying, and what the children are struggling with.

Deciding How to Nudge

No matter where students are in their thinking, there are many ideas they understand and many they do not yet understand. They may also have particular struggles, like ideas they are actively trying to make sense of, explanations they are trying to articulate, or representations they are trying to construct. They may also be struggling with each other, with negotiation and authority. Once the teacher has a picture of this landscape, it is time to decide how to respond and that decision includes two things:

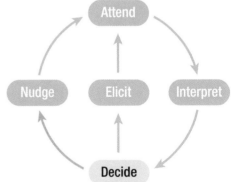

- What should I focus students' attention on to help them grow?
- What should I say to accomplish this?

We know from the transcript of Sofia's conference that she decided to focus students' attention on how they might communicate or represent their thinking for someone else to understand. She did this with two questions that we will look at more closely in the next section. In contrast, if Monica decided how to respond instructionally to her students, it was not in that moment. Her students also could have grown the way they represented their strategy, but by walking away, Monica missed the opportunity to focus students on engaging in this mathematical practice.

Certainly, representing mathematical thinking is not the only possible focus for a conference, and Sofia's questions are not the only way to get there. Deciding what to focus on and how is challenging work. We will dig deeply into these decisions in Chapter 4, when we look at types of nudges and the various moves teachers can use to nudge student thinking. Before we get there, we need to understand how a nudge works.

Nudging . . . and Listening Again

Nudging is what teachers do to push student thinking forward. It is not the same as telling or modeling, which we might more commonly do in a literacy conference. Instead, a nudge points students in a productive direction and creates space for them to grow. The nudge has four critical features:

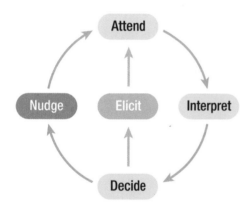

1. Nudges are initiated by the teacher to advance students' mathematical thinking, engagement in mathematical practice, or collaboration.
2. Nudges are responsive to elicited student thinking.
3. Nudges are taken up by students.
4. Nudges maintain student ownership and sense-making.

Let's examine each of these features by looking again at the nudge from Sofia's conference with Vanessa and Orlando (the full transcript of this conference can be found on page 3).

All four features of a nudge can be seen in this nudge from Sofia's conference with Vanessa and Orlando.

SOFIA: OK. And how would you go and explain that to somebody else? Is there a way to draw a picture or explain it in a way for somebody else to understand?

ORLANDO: I guess we could draw a picture . . . somehow. Like we, instead of—.

VANESSA *(interrupting)*: Oh, yeah, 6 circles with 12 inches in them . . . plus the remainder of 5.

ORLANDO *(overlapping):* Yeah, yeah, that's what I was thinking! Yeah, you could do that to explain it!

SOFIA: Very interesting. I'm going to come back and check that out.

Initiated by the Teacher

The teacher selects what she believes is the most productive focus for the conference. The nudge might focus on advancing students' mathematical thinking by supporting their conceptual understanding or helping them to develop a strategy for tackling a task. The nudge might focus on supporting students' engagement in mathematical practices, particularly in communicating, justifying, representing, or modeling thinking. Finally, the nudge might focus on building students' capacity to collaborate effectively by supporting their negotiation and communication with each other. Each of these is a meaningful, rich focus for a conference, going beyond whether the work is merely complete or correct.

The teacher initiates the nudge by pivoting the conference to focus on one of these areas. Sofia accomplishes this by shifting from asking questions about what Vanessa and Orlando have already done to asking them two questions about what they might do next. In this case, Sofia offers two possible directions, both of which center on promoting the students' engagement in mathematical practices: communication and representation.

Responsive to Elicited Student Thinking

The nudge depends on all the information gathered and interpreted in the first part of the conference. We cannot know what the focus of the nudge will be before we confer; it depends entirely on what we learn when we elicit student thinking at the beginning of the conference. This is the essence of responsive instruction and what makes planning for conferences challenging.

In our example, through all of the elicited and probed thinking, the students demonstrated a solid conceptual understanding of the strategy they had developed. But although their oral explanation was complete, they had scant written evidence. Sofia nudged them to capture their thinking so that it could be shared and understood by others. She could not have known this particular nudge would advance their thinking before she had the opportunity to hear that thinking.

Taken Up by Students

Students play a critical role in the conference. Teachers initiate the nudge, but for it to be successful, students must take it up. Consider how this happens with Sofia, Vanessa, and Orlando. Sofia offers the students two ideas for how they could focus on mathematical practices, through explanation or through representation. Orlando takes up the idea of representing their thinking through a drawing and chooses *not* to take up the notion of explaining. Indeed, explanation never comes up again. Once Orlando takes up drawing, he and Vanessa work together to shape that idea, and we can see in their overlapping speech that this is an idea that now belongs to them.

At this point in the conference the teacher must attend closely to how students respond to determine if they are taking up the nudge and making it their own. Sofia's conference would have ended very differently if Orlando had simply said, "I guess," and conversation stopped. The nudge is a shared project of the teacher and the students, and we cannot know if the nudge has been effective until we see how students respond.

Maintain Student Ownership and Sense-Making

The nudge is not direct instruction and it is not modeling. Students must construct their own meaning as they engage in mathematics. The nudge must strike a balance between pointing students down a productive pathway and not holding their hands as they attempt to walk down it. Notice that Sofia asks her students if they could draw a picture, but at no point does she indicate what kind of picture it should be. The nature of the picture comes entirely from the students. They could have created any number of pictures, by, say, using a number line, or drawing rulers, tally marks, or cubes. But we know that the picture that made the most sense to Vanessa and Orlando used circles with the numeral 12 inside to represent the inches in each foot, because this is the representation they created for themselves. They continued to own their work and make sense of the mathematics, and Sofia got to learn something more about their thinking by seeing how they made sense through a representation. The key to achieving this kind of continued ownership and sense-making is a truly open-ended question, one where any number of productive answers are possible and students have authentic choices.

There is much more to be said about how to confer with students, and in the coming chapters we will investigate the stages in the conferring process more closely. In Chapter 3, we will drill down into the cycle that surrounds eliciting and interpreting student thinking. In Chapter 4, we will expand on the nudge by looking at five specific types of nudges and teacher moves you can use to nudge student thinking forward. But first, let's take a moment to consider how conferring fits into your classroom and how you can set the stage for successful conferring. This is the focus of Chapter 2.

COMMON QUESTION

How long should a conference take?

The time it takes to confer varies quite a bit. It can take as little as one minute if students offer their thinking readily, the nudge is clear, and students take it up quickly. Sofia's conference took less than ninety seconds. Some conferences, however, require lots of back-and-forth as students make meaning out of the task, explain thinking, work out ideas, or negotiate. In these cases, conferring can take as long as ten minutes. Most conferences, however, fall in between, taking approximately three to five minutes. You can learn a lot about what students are thinking in just a few minutes, and if you choose the right kind of nudge, this last part of the conference can take just a fraction of a minute.

REFLECTING ON YOUR OWN PRACTICE

In this chapter we've examined examples of conferences and one example of an interaction that is not yet a conference. Take a moment to reflect on your own practice of talking with students while they work.

- In what ways do math conferences sound like your interactions with students during work time? In what ways are they different?
- When and how do you currently elicit and probe student thinking?
- What time do you have in your math structures for conferring, or how could you make time?
- What aspects of your own interactions with students during math would you like to grow?

2

Setting the Stage:
Creating the Conditions for Conferring

J
ust as conferring is one part of the readers' and writers' workshop and could not be implemented in isolation, conferring in mathematics must take place on a broader instructional stage. As teachers, we hope to talk with students about their thinking as they struggle with big ideas and ways of thinking mathematically—in the midst of this kind of grappling there is quite a lot to talk about. But if tasks or expectations in the classroom don't demand deep thinking, we're left with thin conversations about answers. So, what does it take to create a mathematical environment ripe for conferring?

In this chapter, we will examine two crucial ways to set the stage for conferring: choosing rich tasks that generate rich thinking, and setting norms for engaging in collaborative, sense-making math. Rich math tasks create space for students to struggle with concepts,

develop strategies, make mistakes and connections, and engage in math practices. In the messiness of developing understanding through problems, we can have interesting and fruitful conversations with students about their thinking while that thinking is still forming. These are prime moments for nudging students down a productive pathway. The right task creates these opportunities and in this chapter, we'll look at what makes such a task.

Norms are the established expectations and ways of working in classrooms. For students to engage in conferring with us, they need to hold certain expectations about what their role is as problem solvers and what the teacher's role is in supporting their work. Teachers and students need to negotiate norms for how to collaborate productively, what quality work looks and sounds like, and how to learn from struggle and disagreement. Children are our partners in conferring and we need a shared understanding of what this work is. In this chapter, we will look at norms that support conferring and consider how you might set the stage in your own context.

Choosing Rich Tasks

Although students have always been asked to solve problems in math classrooms, in the past these problems have shared some features that make them less productive for learning and discussion. These problems typically have a single prescribed procedure for solving them and a single correct answer, which all students were expected to mirror. Success was defined by the uniformity of students' work, and any talk was often limited to the reporting and evaluation of answers. This is a desiccated version of mathematics; with just the withered husk of procedures and answers there is not much to discuss.

In life, mathematics is messy and full of authentic questions and choices. Standing in the grocery aisle, you may have found yourself comparing boxes of cereal and asking yourself, *Which one is the better value?* Or perhaps you were thinking toward the week ahead, trying to estimate how much milk you and your family might need and comparing that to the price for different-size containers. You likely had to improvise a process, decide how precise you needed to be to be confident in your purchase, and do some flexible mental calculations. There are many ways you might have arrived at a sensible, defensible solution. If you were standing in that grocery aisle with a companion, you might think aloud about your decision and even solicit how they might decide: "How much milk do you think we drink in a day? How many days will it take us to drink a half-gallon carton or a full gallon?

How many days until each carton expires? What's the difference in price?"
The factors they consider might change your process and how you think, as
when your companion points out that it might be better to overestimate than
be forced to come back to the store midweek. This is what rich math looks
like, the ordinary and yet complex problems we face every day as we navigate the real world. Our challenge as teachers is to bring this lively, intercon-
nected, dynamic experience of mathematics to students through rich tasks.

What Is a Rich Task?

What makes a task rich depends in part on your students' daily experiences,
what your students already understand, and what they are ready to learn.
However, rich tasks share several features that can guide you when selecting
and writing problems for your students:

1. Rich tasks are open-ended, encouraging multiple solutions.
2. They allow students to struggle and make sense of important mathematical ideas.
3. They require justification and the use of other mathematical practices.

Open-Ended and Encourage Multiple Solutions

As with our milk problem, math tasks should have multiple ways for arriving at
a solution. The most challenging mathematical work is figuring out what pathways make sense. *How* to solve the problem often *is* the problem. The Common Core's Standards for Mathematical Practice call these solution pathways,
and the need to determine a pathway, rather than having a pathway provided,
makes tasks more demanding and authentic. Students must make choices, consider what they already know and how the current task compares to ones they
have seen or solved before, and be willing to try and test their ideas.

Often the most interesting problems have not only multiple ways to
solve them but multiple answers. Consider the difference between the following three problems:

What is double 3?	We have 6 strawberries and want to share them so that you and I get the same number. How many can we each have?	We have some strawberries and decide to share them so you and I each get the same number. How many strawberries might we have? How many would we each get?

All of these problems center on doubles and two equal groups. The first problem is the most closed, with a single answer and poising most students to think about 3 + 3 as a fact. The second problem is a more open-ended task. We can imagine students might go about solving it in a variety of ways, such as using a known addition fact, passing out manipulatives into two groups, thinking of a die arrangement of 6 and seeing 3 on each side, or thinking about half of 6. But if we open this task up to multiple answers, we get something like the last task. In this final task, students can solve the problem multiple—and in this case, infinite—times, each time thinking about what qualities make a solution. For instance, students might start with thinking that we have 4 strawberries and each get 2, perhaps by holding up 2 fingers on each hand. They might then look at their hands and think that we could have 10 strawberries and each get 5, as they see the 5 fingers on each hand. But what else is possible? Solving the problem repeatedly offers students a reason to look for patterns and develop greater efficiency. But most importantly, it centers the big mathematical idea at the heart of students' work—in this case, what is a double or an even number and why are they useful for sharing? This is not a question that emerges from doing the first problem, and it may not arise from solving the second either.

All rich tasks need some dimension of multiplicity. Not all tasks need multiple answers, but you can see how much these kinds of tasks offer for students to talk about with you and with each other. When students first encounter math tasks where there are real choices to be made, either in the process they craft or in the potential answers they find, they will often feel a great disequilibrium (Carter 2008). Not knowing just what to do can be uncomfortable, particularly if you expect that you should. But such struggle is a critical part of learning and a feature of rich tasks itself.

Allow Struggle and Sense-Making

Struggle is how we learn. Rich tasks provoke productive struggle (National Council of the Teachers of Mathematics 2014), during which students actively struggle through a problem as they work to make sense of it. This is not the same as being stuck. When students are stuck, they are not making progress. More time will not help. But in productive struggle, students are working in that sometimes herky-jerky way in which we all solve real problems.

With our milk problem, we might have stood in the aisle trying to figure out what the right questions to ask even were, weighing the importance of milk consumption, expiration date, cost, and our own willingness to schlep back to the store if we underestimate. We might try first to ask, "How many ounces of milk do we drink in a day?" before discarding that question as not one we can adequately answer. Then we might better imagine what portion of the gallon seems to disappear each day, measuring it in between our fingers as "about this much." In such a situation, we're doing a lot of cognitive work to find a solution pathway, and if we were working on this task in a classroom, our papers might be blank. But we would still be making progress, even in our struggle, and we would be working to make sense of the relevant mathematics as we search for connections and observations that we can use.

To struggle and actively make sense, students must encounter tasks for which they do not have a ready procedure to execute. Such tasks are in what Vygotsky (1978) called the *zone of proximal development* (ZPD), where tasks are neither so simple they can be completed without much thought nor so hard they cannot be completed with the student's current understanding. Tasks in a student's ZPD can be tackled using what the student knows but require a good stretch to figure them out—and they learn from the process. This means that in sharing a rich task with students, we should not also be sharing how *we* would solve it; if we do so, we rob students of the opportunity to figure that out for themselves.

Rich tasks push students to grapple with big mathematical ideas, search for connections, make mistakes, and constantly ask themselves, *Does this make sense?* A task should support students in moving toward a deeper understanding of an important idea. In choosing or writing a rich task for students, a critical question is, what big idea do I want my students to grapple with? Think about our problems about doubles. Simply remembering the doubles facts is not a big idea, but discovering the properties of even and odd numbers is.

Require Justification and the Use of Other Mathematical Practices

Even if you have an open-ended task that requires struggle and sense-making, students will learn more—and have juicier ideas to talk about—if you explicitly ask them to engage in mathematical practices as part of the task. Mathematical practices are how we engage in mathematics, regardless of the specific concepts with which we are grappling. The Common Core State Standards outlines eight standards for mathematical practice that include justification, critiquing the reasoning of others, modeling, and persevering (Common Core State Standards Initiative 2010). In addition to these standards, math practices include posing mathematical questions and looking at the world with a mathematical lens. These practices position students as doers of mathematics, as creators of knowledge.

Rich tasks must ask that students not just solve them, but use a variety of practices as tools for figuring out a solution, communicating with and convincing others, and generalizing bigger mathematical ideas from individual tasks. This means that an answer alone is never enough. All tasks can and should require justification—a convincing explanation of why the solution makes sense. But individual tasks will lend themselves to some practices more than others; some tasks will inherently lean into making models or posing questions. As teachers, we need to keep the practices collectively in mind and look for opportunities to ask students to engage with them. Students will also invent their own opportunities once these practices become part of their habits for doing mathematics, and we should take their lead. For instance, students may spontaneously pose their own mathematical question following exploration (such as, do doubles go on forever?) or organize their findings into a color-coded pictures to show how doubles grow, if these are shared practices in the classroom.

When writing or modifying a task, you'll want to think about how to make engaging in math practices part of the task. Consider the math practices embedded in the following task.

How can you cut this hexagon to show half?
How do you know when you've shown half? Find as many ways as you can.

The task is open-ended, with multiple solutions. If matched to the right group of students, generating multiple solutions would likely lead to some struggle and the need to think deeply about what it means to be half of a shape that is neither a rectangle nor a circle. But for students to really grapple with the idea of half, they need to do more than generate a few hexagons with lines drawn on them. Students need to share their ideas with others and justify why they work. They need to see others' solutions and critique those that they think do not show half. For instance, students need to prove to one another and to themselves which of the following ideas do and do not show half.

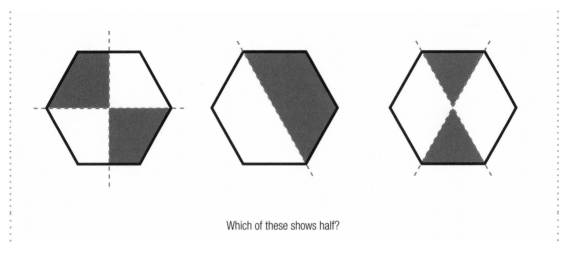

Which of these shows half?

They need to develop models for representing and communicating their ideas, such as cutting out the shapes and folding them to show equal parts or using pattern blocks to model how they might use six triangles as a tool to identify half of a hexagon. And just as importantly, students need to persevere to find solutions beyond the first few that occur to them quickly. There are, in fact, an infinite number of solutions to this task, and the more students find, the closer they will come to identifying a structure for partitioning shapes into two equal regions.

Math practices can be implicit—taken for granted and under the surface of the work we do—but it is often important to make them explicit expectations. This involves making the use of math practices part of the directions, expectations, or questions in a task. In the hexagon task, justification and perseverance are embedded in the directions: "How do you know when you've shown half? Find as many ways as you can." Other prompts that promote and expect the use of mathematical practices include:

- Prompt student to provide reasoning:
  - ▶ Why?
  - ▶ How do you know?
  - ▶ Prove it.
  - ▶ Explain your thinking.
  - ▶ What solutions don't work? Why?

- Prompt student to model:
  - ▶ Show your thinking using pictures, numbers, and/or words.
  - ▶ Create a visual proof for your solution.

▶ How could you show your strategy with a picture, graph, diagram, or objects?

▶ How could you use a number sentence to label what you did?

▶ Color-code your solutions to show the different parts and how they are related.

■ Prompt students to look for structure:

▶ Can you find all the solutions? How do you know when you have found them all?

▶ How can you organize what you've found to help you see patterns?

▶ What patterns do you notice?

▶ Can you predict what other solutions there might be? How do you know?

You may already be in the habit of asking some of these questions; expanding your repertoire will support students in expanding theirs. Adding these kinds of prompts to a task, and making them part of solving a problem, deepens students' learning. Far more important than the answer is how students got there, the ideas they used, the models they created, the mistakes they made, and the patterns they found as a result.

Why Do Tasks Matter for Conferring?

When we confer with students, we are talking about their work—what they are doing, thinking, trying, and wondering. Rich tasks create opportunities for students to think, make mistakes, try again, design strategies, and ask questions. This gives us lots to talk about, and many potential places to be supportive to students. However, if students are merely practicing a procedure repetitively, answering questions with a single correct strategy and answer, or not expected to offer thinking beyond that answer, there is very little to talk about—and, I would argue, very little for students to learn. In selecting tasks, it can be useful to ask yourself what there is to talk about in this task. If you can imagine discussing the strategies students might choose or develop, the patterns in the answers they find, the reasoning behind the solutions that work and don't, or the ways students might create to represent their thinking, then you've likely found a rich task and one that will be rich ground for conferring.

THE ROLE OF RICH TASKS

 In this clip, Faith reflects on the importance of choosing a rich and challenging task. Her second-grade students had been working on developing ideas about place value by counting collections of objects and forming groups of 10. On the previous day, the collections students counted ranged in size from 25 to about 90. Through conferring, Faith realized that this was no longer a rich task for these students because of what they had learned about tens and ones in two-digit numbers. Listen to how this task affected conferring and what task Faith plans to do next.

Setting Norms

For students to engage productively with the kinds of tasks described here, classrooms need to have clear norms for working. Norms communicate what is valued, what mathematics is, and how we engage in mathematics. In the past, norms for working often included being silent, working independently, completing work neatly, replicating the procedure shown by the teacher, and labeling papers with the proper header. Under these norms, mathematics is replication and memorization; speed, correctness, handwriting, and uniformity are valued. We need new norms to support rich, inquiry-based, mistake- and struggle-filled mathematical learning. Norms must be deliberately set in any learning community and they must be constantly reinforced. As you consider how to set norms for your mathematics classroom, it is important to consider students' histories with mathematics. If your students have recently experienced classrooms whose norms valued correctness and uniformity, then you should anticipate that shifting norms will take more time and careful attention.

Types of Norms Math Classrooms Need

Every classroom and community is different, and the specific norms you craft in your classroom will depend on the grade level you teach, your students' experience with rich tasks and sense-making, your own comfort with teaching in this way, and the norms you have in other parts of your day. You may have useful language for how students collaborate, for example, in science, and it would make sense to draw on those norms to help students learn to collaborate in math. In the following sections I outline areas for which every classroom will need norms to support students' mathematical work and your conferring with them. You'll want to think about how to name and describe these norms in your own context.

Teacher and Student Roles

In sensemaking classrooms, students' role is to think, figure out, take risks, make mistakes, revise, have and build ideas, debate, and question. Fundamentally, students are the ones constructing their own knowledge by doing and talking with others. In such a classroom, the teacher's role is to support this work by providing space, tools, tasks, norms, curiosity, observations, questions, and orchestration. This is a far cry from the transmission-based teaching of the past in which the teacher was the expert-teller, and the students were the receptacles into which knowledge was poured. Some students may still expect these roles in math class; they may even become frustrated when a teacher will not just tell them what to do. It is imperative that students receive consistent messages about what their roles are and what to expect from their teacher. If these roles are clearly defined, students come to expect in conferring that their teacher will ask about and be interested in their thinking and their role is to share ideas, ask questions, and struggle together. Without norms about roles, students can feel guarded or insecure when teachers ask questions like, "How do you know?"

Agency

We don't often talk about agency in classrooms, but we should. Agency is a sense of yourself as an actor with power. What powers do you want students to have in your classroom? What can and should they be able to do without you as a gatekeeper? The more agency students have in the classroom, the more power they have over their own mathematical work—which supports their role as sense-makers—and the less they need to come to you for perfunctory permission. Norms for student agency include deciding what materials are needed, accessing those materials and manipulatives, deciding where to work, and choosing partners. For each of these processes, you will need to explicitly teach students what is within their power and how to exercise that power. For instance, if students can choose their own partners, they will need support in naming what makes a productive partnership and reflecting on the choices they make. However, with support students can become independent at a number of decisions, freeing both them and you to do deeper mathematical work. If students have agency to make lots of choices without your permission, then your interactions around mathematics no longer need to be dominated by giving permission. Instead, you can spend your time conferring and focusing on students' thinking.

Collaboration

Collaboration is hard. Perhaps you've been in a meeting in which you thought *I could do this faster on my own.* True collaboration involves a number of skills that students need to learn to be successful. But when successful, collaboration often yields far better results for far more students than independent work. Collaboration is about inclusion, access, talk, debate, building ideas, and revising along the way. When we do math together, everyone learns more. Classrooms need norms for including partners in decision-making and idea-generating, for sharing materials, and for keeping one another on task.

How will students make sure everyone has a voice and no one dominates? How will students share? How will students listen to one another? How will students make sure that their shared work is agreed upon by all members? The class will need to talk about what it means to collaborate, what productive collaborations look and sound like, and the moves they can use to sustain collaboration when it goes astray. The more skilled students become at working together, the more work time you can spend on conferring about mathematical thinking rather than putting out fires around the room. You will always need to spend some time in conferring supporting how students work together, but you want to have time to do more than that. Norms for collaboration enable more mathematical work and more conferring about mathematical learning.

Disagreement

Disagreement is inevitable, and even—mathematically speaking—desirable. It is important to distinguish between disagreements that are about sharing and working together and those that are about mathematics. For interpersonal disagreements, students will need some norms for resolving disputes, like using rock-paper-scissors to decide who will go first in a game. Mathematical disagreements, however, should be resolved through the authority of mathematics itself (Hiebert et al. 1997). Students may be tempted to turn disputes into an occasion for voting (as in, "Who thinks Kevin is right? Now, who thinks I'm right?") or a key moment to seek the authority of the teacher (as in, "He says it's even. I say it's odd. Who's right?"). It is crucial that we as teachers put the resolution of mathematical debates back on students. Students should be tasked with collecting enough evidence to convince themselves and one another of what makes mathematical sense, and only with such evidence can something be said to be true or correct. Resist the urge to tell students that they are correct, even if they beg you (and they will, especially when they are accustomed to teachers serving in the role as the mathematical authority). Instead, the question is, "Are you all convinced?" Such norms help maintain conferring as a place to discuss students' mathematical ideas and develop them, rather than a venue to check answers with the teacher.

Struggle

Productive struggle is how we learn. In mathematics, struggle is sometimes viewed as a sign of weakness, rather than an avenue to strength. Struggle should be positioned in math classrooms as a normal and valued part of the learning process (Hiebert and Grouws 2007). Naming this feeling—that you don't yet understand, that you're unsure, but trying something—can be useful for all students. Struggle is often uncomfortable, and that discomfort, along with the sense that others probably aren't feeling this way, can lead students to try to avoid the very state that will lead to deeper understanding. But by naming explicitly the role that struggle plays in learning, you can create a classroom environment that encourages students to take risks, make mistakes, express confusion, ask questions, and revise their thinking—each of which moves learners toward understanding in productive ways. Conferring is a support for this struggle, a way teachers keep it productive rather than letting it lapse into being stuck.

Quality Work

Students need to know what quality work looks and sounds like, and this will vary widely by grade level. Norms for quality need to be broad enough that they allow for a diversity of strategies and approaches to recording thinking. Students will benefit from seeing examples of quality work highlighted for them throughout the year, as their work develops and new mathematical ideas are explored. When discussing what makes quality work with students, be sure to focus on features such as clarity, evidence, and completeness and what tools students used to achieve them. For instance, students may make their process *clear* by using arrows or numbers to indicate sequence, using precise vocabulary, combining pictures and numbers, or labeling the different parts of their solution. Paying attention publicly to what makes quality work in your classroom will support students in growing the quality of their own work over time. Conferring is then a space in which teachers can support students in attending to quality and hold them accountable to making work clear, complete, and convincing.

Establishing Norms

Establishing and maintaining productive mathematical norms is a topic far too large for this book to fully address. It is crucial to note that norms are not simply stated in the first few weeks of class and then considered established. Norms are a constant project in any classroom, with the heaviest focus at the beginning of the year. In the first six weeks of school, you will need to do explicit work to name the norms in your classroom, probably recording them on a chart that can be a visible reference for all (as in Figure 2.1). But more important than this chart is the work you do to highlight the ways in which students are beginning to engage with these norms. Students learn what is valued in our classrooms by what we focus attention and time on. Take time to dwell on the smallest efforts students make toward collaborating productively, making decisions about tools, recording thinking, or taking risks. Highlight publicly what students are doing and why it is important for learning.

Norms are a two-way street. We work to establish norms to enable math teaching, but also, as we teach, we are reinforcing and refining how students engage in norms. Conferring can happen because of the norms we establish, and as we confer with students, we have opportunities to promote norms around collaboration, struggle, disagreement, and work quality. Norms support teaching, and teaching supports norms. As you teach, you are sending

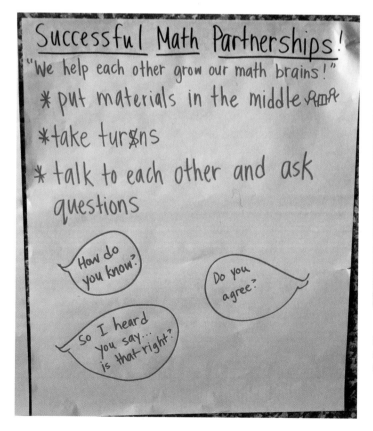

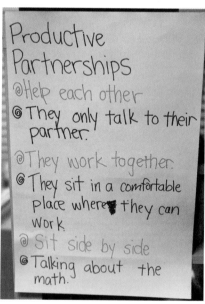

FIGURE 2.1 Examples of classroom charts reinforcing collaboration norms from a second-grade class and a fourth-grade class

messages about what is expected and valued in your classroom, and those messages should be aligned to the norms you have told students explicitly. For instance, if you've told students that mathematical disagreements are resolved by using mathematical evidence, when you talk to students who disagree, you can support this norm by helping them to develop and discuss evidence, rather than declaring who is right. The more often you use time to coach students through such mathematical disagreements, the better able students will be to resolve these debates independently and the less they will look to you to be the mathematical authority.

Why Do Norms Matter for Conferring?

Conferring is part of the two-way street of norming; norms support conferring, and conferring can support norms. Part of the importance of norms is purely practical. When students are relatively independent and can solve disputes and make decisions about materials without your intervention or permission, you are able to spend your valuable instructional time talking about mathematics. Conferring takes time and sustained attention. Frequent interruptions to manage students' behavior or access to manipulatives makes it challenging to focus on conferring, what students are thinking, and how you might nudge that thinking forward.

Just as important as this practical dimension to norms are the messages about what is valued. Conferring is about listening, deeply and genuinely, to what students are thinking right now, giving it your full attention and, in doing so, communicating how important that thinking is. Conferring is most successful when that message—that students' thinking, ideas, and questions matter—is aligned to the surrounding norms in the classroom. Conferring focuses on supporting students in generating ideas, recording thinking, choosing strategies, working with others, coming to consensus, communicating reasoning, and making connections. Conferring makes sense in a larger classroom environment focused on processes like those described in this chapter: collaborating, struggling, resolving disagreements, making decisions, and developing quality work. Furthermore, conferring can then be used to support these norms. For instance, when conferring about how students might represent their thinking, you can support norms around quality work by asking students how they can make their representation clear to others. Conferring can help norms move from a poster on the wall to the regular, lived experience of doing mathematics.

COMMON QUESTIONS

My curriculum doesn't have a lot of rich tasks. What can I do?

Most curriculum materials include tasks that can be modified to be rich, by making the tasks more open ended and encouraging the use of math practices. When selecting tasks from within the resources you have, start by looking for tasks that ask students to think about ideas that they have some mathematical tools for but have not yet fully mastered. Tasks that ask students to simply practice something they know well to become faster at a procedure have little potential to be rich tasks. Often (and inequitably) the richest tasks are located in sections for challenge or differentiating for "high" students. These tasks are rarely offered to all students, but they should be. Often these tasks, too, will require some modification, but they can be a fruitful starting point. There are also many supplementary resources available with great tasks, and I have included some of my favorites for further reading in the appendix. These resources can serve as both banks of tasks to choose from and models for writing your own. I have frequently found that browsing through rich tasks helps me generate ideas for writing tasks that are more tailored to what my students need than anything I could have found in a book.

Can I shift my norms midyear? How?

Yes! Shifting norms midyear is certainly more work than establishing norms at the beginning of the year, and it takes some deliberate efforts to get students to come along for the ride. First, it is important to explain to students why you want to shift the norms the class currently has. Bring students on board for the shared project and be open about your own teaching work. You may feel vulnerable, nervous, and uncertain. This is your own struggle and it is where learning happens! Second, take on a few key norms at a time. Think about what norms you have in other parts of your day that you can work to extend to math time. For instance, if students have the agency to choose their own books in reading, it would make sense that they can choose their own manipulatives in math. Make the connection for students between these two ways of putting them in charge of making decisions about their learning. Third, recognize for yourself and for your students every tiny step toward the norms you hope to see. Notice these moments aloud, thank students for taking risks or trying something new, and reflect on the specific things you are all doing to move toward a more inquiry-based, process-focused approach. Remember that norms are a constant process, and celebrating the journey will only serve to reinforce the value of growth and struggle.

REFLECTING ON YOUR OWN PRACTICE

As you think about setting the stage for conferring in your math classroom, the following guiding questions may help you reflect on what you need to do to provide students with rich tasks and establish productive norms. Think about both what your vision is for your classroom and what concrete steps you can take now to move toward it.

Guiding Questions for Selecting, Revising, or Crafting Tasks

- What resources do you have access to that may contain rich tasks? Where are those rich tasks?
- What kinds of modifications might the tasks in your resources need to become rich? Do they need to be opened up? Do math practices need to be made more explicit?
- What rich tasks do you already use with your students? How could you modify them to create new tasks?
- What colleagues might be interested in working with you to modify or write rich tasks? Your grade-level team? A coach?

Guiding Questions for Crafting Your Own Norms

- How will you communicate your role and students' roles?
- How do you want students to manage their own needs in the classroom? What decisions do you want them to make independently?
- How will you give students access to materials? How will you teach students to make use of these resources?
- What do you want collaboration to look like? What is the language of collaboration?
- How will you talk about what it means to work together? How will you talk about sharing, dominating, inclusion, and exclusion?
- What tools do you want students to use to resolve disputes?
- How will you generate mathematical debate? How will you help students make meaningful arguments? How will you support students in determining when they feel convinced?
- How will you name struggle as a valued part of learning?
- What do you want students to do when they are struggling?

- For students in your grade and context, what will a quality explanation sound like? What will quality written work look like? What are the features of quality you want students to be able to see and name?
- What activities can you engage students in at the beginning of the year that will give students the opportunity to try on these norms and you the opportunity to make them a focus?

Guiding Questions for Reflecting on Your Existing Norms

- What role are you currently playing in your math classroom? How does it differ from the role you play in other parts of the day? Why does it differ? What would you like your role to look like in math? What concrete steps could you take to revise your role?
- What role do students currently play in your math classroom? How does that role differ from the roles they play in other parts of the day? Why? What role would you like students to play in math? How might you encourage students to revise their roles?
- What are students empowered to do independently? What kinds of decisions are you the gatekeeper for?
- Are there ways to transfer more authority to students so you have more time to focus on instruction? What procedures would you need to put in place? What would students need to practice to take this authority on?
- How are students collaborating with one another now? How could they get more power out of working together? What skills do they need to learn?
- What do students do now when they struggle or make a mistake? How would you like that to change? What do they need from you to make those changes?
- Who talks and who doesn't? Why? What role are your current norms playing in encouraging some students to participate more than others?
- What does student written work look like now? How do students currently justify their answers? How would you like that work to grow?
- What reflections on your norms would you like to share with students? What feedback might you want to collect from students on how math class is going for them? How could you open up conversation about your norms with the aim of moving them toward your vision?

3

Eliciting and Interpreting:
What Are They Doing?

Every conference is built on what students are doing and thinking in the moment. When we approach students at work, we're coming in midstream. Because we're joining work that's already begun, our first task is to understand the progress students have made. But students rarely volunteer everything we need to know spontaneously, so teachers need to ask questions. The goal of this first stage of the conference is to figure out what students understand, what they misunderstand or do not yet understand, and how they are putting their ideas to work.

In this chapter, we will first examine the stance teachers bring to conferring and how that stance impacts the interaction that follows. Stance sets the tone and purpose of conferring and impacts the roles teachers and students play in the interaction. Some stances are counterproductive,

and in my own research I have found that shifting a teacher's stance toward conferring is a key step in making conferring more productive for student learning. We'll look at stances that work against the goal of advancing student thinking, and then unpack one powerful stance that is consistently and pervasively fruitful.

Then we will take a close look at the work of eliciting student thinking and how we make sense of what students are doing. Eliciting is the heart of conferring. The goal is to learn what students understand, do not yet understand, misunderstand, and what they are trying—to truly get inside their thinking. This is a lot to do in a couple of minutes. When we approach students to confer, what should we pay attention to? What questions or moves can elicit student thinking? How do we put the information together to form an interpretation that's useful and accurate? In this chapter, we'll address each of these questions and look at several examples of how teachers elicit student thinking with their own students.

Stance

We don't often talk about stance, or the attitudes and beliefs that affect how we approach our teaching, but it quietly and consistently changes the course of every interaction we have with students. Experienced teachers take their stance for granted; it is habit, unstated, and practiced constantly. Stance is visible from the moment a teacher approaches a group of students to confer. Sometimes the words sound like the teacher is trying to support student thinking, but the tone, body language, and pace of the interaction say something very different. Students read and respond to these cues.

In my work with teachers, I have seen several stances used when conferring—each defined by a different purpose. Some of these stances prove to be unproductive, and we're going to start by looking at those. Then we'll close this section by examining the most powerful and fruitful stance for conferring, one of genuine curiosity.

Unproductive Stances

Unproductive stances focus on something other than student *thinking* and instead center on students' behavior, the assignment, or the answer. These stances are motivated by different purposes, and they often lead to a different pace of conversation and a great deal more teacher control. When teachers take these stances, they are unlikely to be able to nudge student thinking forward. We have all taken these stances before, and perhaps been frustrated by the results. Finding a more productive pathway begins by recognizing what doesn't work and why.

Management

When a teacher approaches conferring with a management stance, she focuses on getting students on task, and, often, catching kids being off task. The words may be, "What are you working on?" but the tone can be one of accusation, as in, "I know you're not working on anything." It is difficult for a conversation to escape this kind of opening and then become productively focused on student thinking. The pace of this kind of conference tends to be one of short, clipped questions—a sort of interrogation. Teachers using this stance are attempting to exert control over what students are doing, which can sometimes take the form of managing students' bodies, telling them where to sit, what to touch (or not), who to look at, and whose job it is to perform different kinds of work. Management is certainly necessary in every classroom, but using conferring as a cloak for management can lead students not to trust your questions as genuine inquiries into their thinking. This mistrust will undermine conferring in your classroom. Furthermore, exerting a great deal of control over how the work should look reduces students' choices and agency. Better to manage behaviors directly by reminding students of norms, or, when possible, to assume that students *are* being productive and ask them honestly about their work.

Completion

Teachers take a completion stance when the central purpose of the conference is to get students through the task to an answer. It is crucial to remember that students learn from the process of doing mathematics, not from the answer itself. Hustling students through the process to the answer undermines learning. When focused on completion, teachers tend to ask closed questions about procedures or resort to just telling kids what to do to get to the answer. The teacher will often have a predetermined pathway in mind and use questions to direct students down it, like a human manual providing steps, one by one. These questions might start with, "What do we do next?" If students answer incorrectly, the teacher might say, "Is *that* what we do?" with the clear implication that the student is wrong and should guess again. You can see how quickly this stance moves away from what students are thinking to guessing what the teacher wants to hear. These conferences almost always end with the students arriving at a correct answer, but they may not understand what they did. Their *work* may have been advanced, but not their *thinking*. Don't fool yourself; these conferences don't teach.

Fix-It

A fix-it stance may start by asking students about their thinking, but the teacher is looking for errors, not understanding. The teacher's purpose is to identify mistakes in the process and correct them, performing pinpoint repair. Although one central role of conferring is to uncover and address misconceptions, this should not be confused with fixing. Fixing is about making it right; addressing misconceptions is about building understanding. There are two problems with a fix-it stance that bear discussing. First, fixing makes each conference a hunt for mistakes, and questions can take on a tone of testing students. This makes conferring feel like an oral examination rather than a constructive conversation about thinking. It undermines the value of mistakes as tools for learning. Fixing turns the teacher into a mathematical policeman—not a productive (or, honestly, an enjoyable) role. The second major problem with the fix-it approach is that it leaves you with nothing to say to students who understand. What if there is nothing to fix? I have often heard that conferring with students when they understand and are on a productive pathway is the hardest for many teachers, and I suspect this is because it is easier to fix than build understanding. But focusing on understanding is far more productive, as we shall see.

The Productive Stance: Genuine Curiosity Toward Student Thinking

The most productive stance a teacher can take in conferring, and, indeed, in all of teaching, is one of genuine curiosity toward student thinking. Here's the thing: kids do amazing, surprising, creative, and deeply intriguing things. It is fascinating how they understand mathematical ideas, and it is just as wondrous how they misunderstand these ideas. They are fonts of unexpected connections and inventive solutions. If you provide students with rich tasks and create productive norms for work, your students will do what they do when reading the best books or writing about their lives—what Eleanor Duckworth (2006) called the "having of wonderful ideas." Get curious about what your kids are doing! And not fake curious—*genuinely* curious about their wonderful ideas.

What Genuine Curiosity Looks Like

Genuine curiosity has several hallmarks. The tone of the questions sends the message that the teacher just wants to know more about the student's ideas. Curiosity leads to open, authentic questions. Teachers who are curious tend to ask questions they don't know the answer to and make few assumptions about what students are thinking. Even when there is written work or manipulatives and the teacher has an idea of what students have done, a curious teacher will ask, because sometimes students surprise us. For instance, if you notice students holding a ruler against a table during a measurement task, it may seem obvious that the students are figuring out its length. But asking how they are using the ruler and what it tells them may reveal that they are counting how many rulers long the table is, rather than using standard units. This could open up conversation about whether it is the ruler or the foot that matters, perhaps a good question for the whole class to grapple with.

Curious teachers are patient, providing time for students to think about what they want to say, formulate their ideas into words, misspeak, and self-correct. Curious teachers resist sending signals to students that they need to hurry up, knowing that thinking is slow work and patience reduces anxiety. Curious teachers try to put themselves in the minds of their students, looking for how their students are making sense. Even misconceptions make sense in some way, and curious teachers look for that sense before they try to unravel it.

When teachers are genuinely curious about their students' thinking, several things happen in conferring that are important for student learning. First, children feel safe to share new, shaky, and still-forming ideas, and they come to see their own voice as valued. When we ask honestly, "What are you trying?," students feel that their efforts and ideas are the center of our collective work—perhaps the most important message we can send to our students. Second, a genuinely curious stance promotes staying in the moment with students. The unproductive stances we examined all focus on what the teacher *wants* to see—students on task, finishing, getting the correct answer—rather than what students *are* doing and then use the conversation to drive toward the teacher's goal. A genuinely curious stance focuses instead on understanding what students are doing, how they are making sense of their work, and what *they* are trying to accomplish. Staying in the moment turns out to be an important lever for making conferring productive for student learning.

Finally, curiosity means that teachers aren't trying to control student thinking, just understand it. When conferring doesn't work, it is often because teachers use moves to try to control students' ideas, strategies, recording, explanations, bodies, and next steps. Taking over student thinking undermines the importance of their ideas and makes the teacher's thinking the most valued. Furthermore, students may not understand how and why the teacher's processes work. Telling students that they should do it the teacher's way robs them of mathematical authority and may disconnect them from sense-making. Fundamentally, we, as teachers, must approach all students with the belief that what they are doing makes sense to them in some way, and we have to find that sense to grow it.

Cultivating Curiosity

One way to cultivate a genuinely curious stance toward student thinking is by looking at student work with colleagues and practicing. Look at a pile of student work—from any students—and ask yourself, *What does each student seem to understand? What interesting things did they do? What were they trying out? What did they invent? What connections did they make? What's surprising? What's confusing? What does the work make me wonder?* Practice not judging the quality of the work or the student. Practice not trying to fix anything or deciding what the child needs. Just marvel. Curiosity requires practice, but soon it becomes second nature, with profound benefits for your students.

Try being curious with the three examples of student work shown in Figure 3.1, from fourth graders subtracting 129 T-shirts from an inventory of 381 T-shirts. Ask the questions:

- What does each student seem to understand?
- What interesting things did the students do?
- What were they trying out? What did they invent?
- What connections did they make?
- What's surprising? What's confusing?
- What does the work make you wonder?

Don't worry about what to do to fix mistakes or what instruction the child needs next. Just notice and ask questions. What could this work tell you about the child who made it? What do you wish you could ask them?

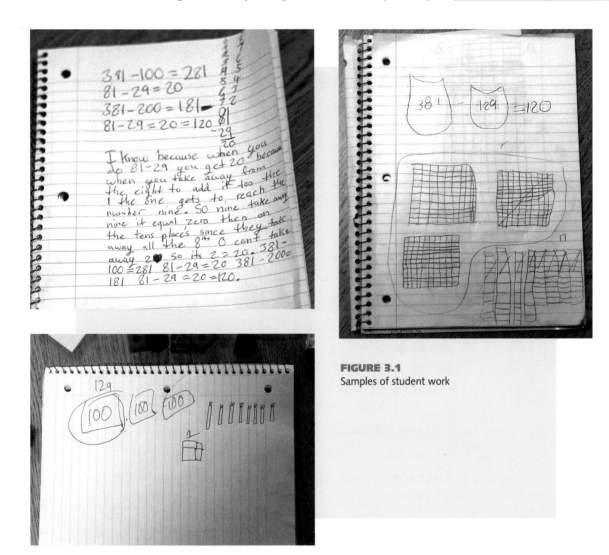

FIGURE 3.1
Samples of student work

Eliciting and Interpreting Student Thinking

If stance is the heart of conferring, pumping the lifeblood of each interaction, then eliciting student thinking is the skeleton, the framework that holds it up and gives it integrity. Conferring centers on student thinking, so the first thing we need to do is surface that thinking, in students' own words. Let's look at an example of a second-grade teacher, Marta, starting to confer with two students, Manuel and Keenan, by eliciting their thinking. The students were working on the following task, set on their school's farm:

> There are 60 chickens in our farm. Some of the chickens are in the coop and some are in the yard. How many might be in the coop? How many might be in the yard?

When Marta approached the two children, they had a rekenrek, or 10×10 bead frame, on their table, along with a piece of paper and two pencils. The beads had been moved and they had written some things down. Marta sat down at the table and began to confer.

MARTA: Hi, guys, what are you trying?

KEENAN: We're using the rekenrek.

MANUEL: Yeah, we made 60.

MARTA: Where is your 60?

MANUEL: (*Points to the rekenrek where 6 rows of 10 beads have been pushed to one side, and then counts the rows aloud*) 1, 2, 3, 4, 5, 6.

MARTA: Oh, I heard you count "1, 2, 3, 4, 5, 6" (*pointing to the rows*). How did you know it was 60?

KEENAN: 'Cause each one is 10.

MANUEL: Yeah, like 10, 20, 30, 40, 50, 60.

MARTA: OK, you counted them as 6 tens, and so you knew that was 60. Is that right?

MANUEL AND KEENAN: Yeah.

MARTA: So, why did you make 60?

KEENAN: For the chickens.

MARTA: What's happening with the chickens in this story?

KEENAN: There're 60 chickens and some are inside and some are outside.

MANUEL: Yeah, but we don't know. We don't know how many.

In the first minute or so of this interaction, Marta has done several important things that help her to learn about Manuel and Keenan's thinking at that moment. She has asked questions and used prompts to encourage the students to tell her what they are doing, such as "What are you trying?" and "What's happening in this story?" She probed the reasoning behind what they were doing, when she asked, "How did you know it was 60?" when the student counted by ones instead of tens. She checked her own understanding of students' thinking by revoicing, when she said, "OK, you counted them as 6 tens, and so you knew that was 60. Is that right?"

Using this collection of moves, Marta has surfaced a lot of thinking. She can use the information she has gathered to form an interpretation of where these students are and what they understand. For instance, she could now interpret that these students understand the story that they are engaged with, that they understand the relationship between 60 and 6 tens and how to model that on the rekenrek, and that these students seem to be working together on the task. She can also interpret that they are unsure about what comes next in solving this task, though they have all the tools for developing a strategy.

The rest of this chapter will focus on what Marta has done, eliciting student thinking and forming an interpretation of that thinking. We will consider what to pay attention to when you first approach students to confer, what moves you can use to elicit and probe, and how you can monitor and test your own developing interpretations. You'll find links to videos later in the chapter that show how eliciting can look, and you can use these to try out interpreting student thinking.

Approaching Students at Work: What to Pay Attention To

Imagine your students at work around the classroom. They might be clustered in pairs or groups of three or four, sitting at tables or maybe some are on the carpet. You've given them a rich task to work on, and they've gotten started, some with gusto and others more hesitantly. It's time to begin conferring to find out what sense your students are making of the task, what ideas are bubbling up, what challenges and confusions they are confronting and then to provide them with some support to deepen their thinking. You scan the classroom, decide where to dive in, and approach a pair of students. As you walk up to their table and take a seat, you probably know next to nothing about where they are in their work at this moment. Learning about students' thinking efficiently means paying attention to all the clues available, starting with your walk to the table.

So, what should you pay attention to? In the few seconds that you have approaching students, sitting down, and taking a breath before you launch into eliciting, you'll want to notice a few aspects of students' work that might help you ask more focused eliciting questions and get a hunch about what's going on with their work. Not all of these may apply on any given day—it depends on the task students are working on—but it will help to take a quick inventory of the following:

- **COLLABORATION.** Does it look like everyone in the group is included in the work? Pay attention to how bodies are arranged and whether anyone is being physically blocked out of conversation or access to the materials, like manipulatives or paper and pencil.

- **THE WORK.** Where are the students doing their thinking work? Students might be using paper and pencil, fingers, or any one of a buffet of manipulatives and tools. They may be acting the mathematics out in some way. Noticing where the thinking is happening can help you see how students have entered the task and what understanding they already have of it. Also notice what's not being used. They may, for example, be organizing tons of cubes but have a blank paper.

- **TONE.** Are students frustrated? Angry? Eager? Excited? Confused? Pay attention to the tone and volume of voice students are using with one another and then with you. Watch facial expressions and body language. You'll want to anticipate a different conversation with students who shout that they have something cool to show you than with the group where a student has his face buried in his arms on the table.

- **ORGANIZATION.** Does the work appear to have a system or a plan? Pay attention to how students have created space for their work and how they are keeping track of what they are doing. For instance, for students counting cubes, do they seem to have a way of tracking what's been counted and what is left to count? You might see piles of cubes and wonder about the size of the groups; it matters mathematically if the groups are equal sizes or if they are groups of five, three, or ten.

Take a few seconds to notice these aspects of how students are working. You may want to go further and sit down with the group to observe their work in progress and their interactions before you ask any questions at all. What you learn by attending to the collaboration, work, tone, and organization will give you ideas for the kinds of questions you want to ask to learn more about where the group is and, ultimately, what they might need from you to advance their work.

Moves and Questions to Elicit and Probe

After you have spent a moment observing students at work, it's time to launch into conferring. The central goal is to surface students' thinking so that everyone can see it. This includes what students have already done, how they are thinking about the task, the confusions or challenges they are grappling with, and how they understand one another. When eliciting, you will likely use a combination of general eliciting and probing moves—those that could be used in any conference—and specific eliciting moves targeted to precisely what you are seeing from these students in this moment. Probing students' reasoning has a particular value, because we want to know not just *what* students have done but *why* and *how* they understand it. As you begin to uncover student thinking, you'll want to check your understanding and focus on details that might matter. This includes attending to all the members of a group, not just the most vocal.

General Eliciting Moves: Getting Started

Most conferences open with a general eliciting move. Eliciting is a habit for both teachers and students; over time students come to expect eliciting questions and learn to offer their thinking, though rarely in a complete package. These moves, or some variation, tend to work well as ways to launch conferring:

- What are you working on?
- Tell me about your thinking.
- What are you all thinking?
- How did you get started?
- What are you trying?
- What have you done so far?

Notice how these questions invite students to share work in progress. The emphasis is on ongoing work, rather than completed work. It is not typically useful, for instance, to ask students about their answer as an eliciting question. We want to know about the process, not the endpoint (yet). Conferring occurs most often in the midst of figuring out; that is, in fact, the great potential in conferring. So rather than asking, "What did you get?," these questions focus on what students are trying, working on, or thinking with the full expectation that it might change.

A quick note on another common launching question, "How's it going?" This is a comfortable and friendly question, but in my experience, it is almost always answered by one word: *good.* It does not serve as an eliciting question, but as a conversational move, like "How are you?" and you will have to immediately follow up with an eliciting question like one noted here. However, when you notice a lot of emotion, you might want to start with this question. In these cases, you may get more than the answer "Good," which will give you something to follow up on. You may also want to draw attention to the emotions or tone you notice and ask specifically about it: "I notice you look upset," or "You guys sound frustrated. What's going on?" ■

Following Up

It is critical to bear in mind that eliciting requires follow-up questions. Students will need your questions to scaffold their explanation. Eliciting, beyond serving as a way for you to learn about student thinking, is also an opportunity for students to practice explaining, articulating, and justifying their thinking, which helps students learn (Franke et al. 2009). Your questions help students learn how to do this by indicating where they need to say more. For instance, when you ask students to tell what they are working on, they may simply offer, "We're multiplying," and your follow-up questions will scaffold their explanation to include what they are multiplying, how they are modeling it, and why it makes sense. Do not make assumptions about what students did or what they understand. Ask follow-up questions to explore the gaps in what students have offered. Some useful general eliciting questions or prompts for following up include:

- Say more about that.
- What did you do first?
- What did you do next? And then what did you do?
- Can you show me what you did?
- How did you get that?
- What is happening in this task (or story)?
- What do you understand (about this task)?

These moves encourage students to sequence or add detail to their explanations. At times students will have little ongoing work to describe because the task itself has left them confused about how to get started. Moves like "What is happening in this story?" or "What do you understand about this task?" help students narrate how they are understanding what they have been asked to do, which is critical to getting started and important information for you to have.

Targeted Eliciting Moves: Focusing on Features of the Work

The general talk moves mentioned here can be used in lots of conferences, and many may become routine in your classroom. They help you to begin to uncover what students are doing, but to really understand the specific details of students' work, you will need more targeted moves. Targeted eliciting moves are those that are specific to what students are doing. These moves focus on a specific aspect of students' work and may be so tailored to the moment that they could only be used in a particular conference. These targeted follow-up questions are where curiosity shines. Students are going to offer you incomplete, and sometimes difficult to follow, explanations of what they are thinking or trying. Follow-up questions allow you to pinpoint specific places where you'd like more information. Put your finger on the work and ask questions about the parts. You might notice:

■ **SURPRISING OR ORIGINAL THINKING.** Students might have tried an unexpected strategy, conceived the task in a way others have not, or invented something new. When you see something unanticipated, it is worth asking about.

▶ What were you trying here?

▶ What were you thinking about?

▶ Where did you get this idea?

▶ How is this helping you?

▶ What is your plan?

■ **DIFFERENT COMPONENTS OF THE WORK.** Students might have manipulatives, written work, oral explanations, counting, or other components of their thinking and work. You'll want to ask about the connections between these parts.

▶ How is this connected to this?

▶ Tell me how you're using (your fingers, this equation, a tool or manipulative). How is that helping you?

▶ How does this match what's happening in the story (or task)?

■ **POTENTIAL MISCONCEPTIONS.** You may see areas in students' work that you think indicate a misunderstanding. These are places to ask questions about what students mean, where the work came from, and what it represents.

▶ What does this mean?

▶ Where did this number (or picture or equation) come from?

▶ What does this represent?

■ **GAPS IN THE EXPLANATION OR PLACES WHERE YOU ARE CONFUSED ABOUT WHAT STUDENTS DID.** You may want to support students to sequence their explanation or describe what the different parts of their work represent or where they came from. You might simply want to tell students what you understand about their thinking and where you got confused.

▶ How did you get this? What does this represent?

▶ Where did this come from?

▶ What's happening here?

▶ So, I see that you did this and this, but I'm confused about this part. Can you tell me about that?

■ **ORGANIZATION.** If you have questions about the organization of students' work that came up as you approached the group, you may want to target some questions to this issue.

▶ Tell me about how you're organizing your blocks (or tallies, or findings, or work).

▶ Where did these groups come from? How are you sorting? Why are these grouped together?

▶ How are you organizing your thinking on the page?

▶ How are you keeping track of all the parts (or numbers or groups)?

Targeted follow-up questions are where we get into the nooks and crannies of student thinking and discover their still forming thinking. Beyond what students have done, however, we want to know what understandings are driving those choices. For this we want probing questions.

Probing Moves

Students are apt to answer eliciting questions by describing at some level of detail what they have done. But in the end, no single problem or task is important. Rather, it is the mathematical concepts and practices that underpin the choices students make when tackling tasks that are generalizable to other situations. The why matters. Justification is a central math practice, and probing student reasoning has the twofold purpose of surfacing student understanding for you to see and giving students the opportunity to justify and deepen their thinking (Kazemi and Stipek 2001). Justification is not something students will be able to do without practice, and constructing mathematical arguments takes active work. When we ask students why they did something, they will likely need to think hard about their reasoning before they can put it into words. When you ask why, wait time is critical; let kids do the hard work of constructing a justification in halting, hesitating, and incomplete terms. Many of the questions we ask to probe student reasoning are general and can be used in nearly any context:

■ Why?

■ How do you know?

■ How (or why) did you decide to do that?

■ Why does that make sense?

■ Why does that work?

■ Why did you . . . ?

You can rarely go wrong asking students for their reasoning, but your questions will be most fruitful when you probe in places where you really want to know if and how students understand the mathematical ideas behind their work. For instance, you could ask students who have just explained how they subtracted 9 from 21, "Why?" but you will learn more—and you will ask more focused questions—if you know that you are trying to learn what role students' understanding of place value played in their strategy. Probing draws attention to mathematical ideas and can give you insight into how students think. Probing can also make these ideas the subject of discussion, moving conferring from talking about a particular task (like 23 + 49) to talking about concepts (like place value). There are times when students know a procedure for finding an answer to a task, without understanding why that procedure works. This is crucial information for you to have, and probing questions help shift discussion away from the procedure and toward mathematics.

> ### REFLECTIONS ON PROBING STUDENT THINKING
>
> **3.1** In this clip, Mary reflects on how learning moves to probe students' thinking helped her learn to confer in math in a way that was different from her conferring practice in literacy.

Eliciting and probing are interwoven in the initial stage of conferring. You may ask a few eliciting questions, then probe the reasoning behind what students offer, and return to eliciting what came next. These moves are meant to help you form a mental map of the work you have entered into midstream.

Revoicing and Noticing Aloud

As you elicit and probe, two moves can be powerful for pinpointing student thinking. Revoicing is a tool for checking your own understanding of student thinking. Noticing aloud draws students' attention to details in their work and enables you to ask specific follow-up questions.

REVOICING. Revoicing is just repeating back to students what you have heard them say to you, with a question to check if you have heard them correctly (Chapin, O'Connor, and Anderson 2013), such as, "So, I heard you say . . . Is that right?" or "Let me see if I'm understanding you. You . . . Is that right?" Often students will offer you information about their thinking in nonlinear, halting, or imprecise ways as they work to construct a narrative of their process or reasoning. Revoicing lets you check your own understanding of student thinking. Your revoicing also allows students to hear back in a more concise way their own explanation and can serve as a model for how to refine and revise an explanation to be clearer. They get the opportunity to clarify anything that may be inaccurate, which serves to make their

It is important with revoicing that you say back to students what they have told you, not what you assume. You'll want to refrain from filling in the reasoning for students; instead, revoice and ask why. ■

explanation—and your understanding of it—more complete. Students will often be spurred to add on to this explanation, providing additional details, reasoning, or steps. In this way, revoicing also serves to elicit.

NOTICING ALOUD. Noticing aloud is a powerful and generative strategy for focusing attention, eliciting and probing fine details, and being actively curious. Noticing aloud involves naming for students something specific about their work that you noticed and would like to talk more about. It may be something in their written work, how they used manipulatives or fingers, what they said, or how they are working together. Simply put, noticing aloud sounds like, "I noticed that . . ." typically followed by a question about that specific feature. The question could be probing, such as "Why?" or "What made you do that?" or it could be eliciting, such as "What does that mean?" or "Where did that come from?" or "Tell me more about that." For instance, if you are looking at students' work and you notice that they have erased or made changes, you might say, "I notice that you crossed out $\frac{1}{5}$ and wrote $\frac{2}{5}$ next to it. What made you change your mind?"

Noticing aloud serves several purposes. First, noticing aloud is affirmative. When you state what students have done, it is a fact, not a question. Stating clearly what students have done positions them as competent and makes it more likely that they will talk about the feature you've identified. Second, noticing aloud focuses all attention on an area of student work that might be mathematically fruitful. Narrowing the conversation to one feature can allow you to go deeper. Third, sometimes we don't know exactly what to ask students, but we know where there is potential in their work. Noticing aloud can help us pinpoint that productive place and then ask a general question or ask for more information, such as "Tell me more about that." Finally, noticing aloud is celebratory. It sends the message that their work is worth noticing, fascinating, and complex. If you don't know what to say to students, looking for something interesting to notice aloud and dwell on is a worthy move.

Collaboration: Eliciting and Probing Across the Group

Collaborative mathematics work offers students rich opportunities to cross-pollinate ideas, build on one another's thinking, brainstorm, push each other to articulate and justify, and support risk-taking. However, each of these requires learning. Students do not learn how to listen to each other's thinking, build on each other's ideas, and press one another to explain without being taught—and then expected—to do so. Instead, inequity may develop in the context of group or partner work. One student may take over and box out partners from participation. Two students may talk actively with one another but not leave space for a third to join in. The partnership may devolve into parallel independent work, or no work at all.

When eliciting and probing students' thinking, attend to who answers your questions and the body language of those who do not. When one student repeatedly answers your questions and others remain silent, it can be a signal that either the group is not functioning equitably or that understanding is not shared. You'll want to ask specific questions that elicit and probe student thinking across the partnership to assess how (and whether) the group is working jointly and to what degree students all share an understanding of the task, strategy, or work. When you are talking to the group, be sure that your own body language includes all members, rather than orienting only to the most vocal students. Ask questions of the entire group, and, when you need to draw out quieter members, ask them questions directly. To elicit and probe thinking across the group, you might say:

- What do *you* think?
- What do you think about what she just said?
- Do you agree or disagree? Why?
- What was your idea?
- Tell me about what *you* wrote (or made, did, or thought).
- Why do *you* think that (what your partner just said) makes sense?
- Can you revoice (or retell or say) what you just heard your partner say?
- What are you wondering about what he just said?
- Do you all agree on this strategy? Why?

ELICITING STUDENT THINKING

Like all of conferring, eliciting looks different depending on the interaction. Watch the clips of Mary and Faith eliciting their own students' thinking as they launch into conferring, and consider the following questions:

- What moves is the teacher using to make her students' thinking visible?
- How does the teacher follow up on students' thinking to surface more?
- What targeted moves do you notice?
- How and when does she probe for reasoning?
- How does the teacher engage all students?
- Which moves seem to be the most fruitful?

At the end of each clip, think about your interpretation of the students' thinking. Use the questions in the Forming an Interpretation section to reflect on the evidence surfaced through eliciting.

3.2 In this clip, Faith's second graders were continuing work on taking inventory of classroom materials by organizing them in packs or groups of ten and loose ones to build understanding of place value. These students were counting a bucket of foam geometric solids when Faith began to elicit thinking about their counting.

3.3 In this clip, Faith's second graders were working to solve the problem:

My mom has 20 packs of 10 Halloween pencils and 4 loose ones. How many Halloween pencils does she have? How do you know?

Faith designed this task to push students beyond two-digit numbers while still thinking about tens and ones.

3.4 Mary's fourth-grade students were asked to solve the following task:

The factory has an inventory of 381 small T-shirts. A customer bought 129 small T-shirts. How many small T-shirts are there now?

Mary approached a pair of students she had noticed from across the room that were not collaborating. Notice how Mary uses different kinds of eliciting to uncover what was going on.

These questions create openings for students to participate. Often when we see one student on the outside of the work, it is because that student has been excluded, not that they have failed to participate. Exclusion can happen deliberately, or it can happen incidentally, as when one partner has a clear vision for how to solve the problem and forges ahead alone. By asking eliciting and probing questions across the partnership, we can detect and begin to repair inequitable access to the work. As teachers, we also need to know how each student is thinking and not assume that the thinking of the most vocal student represents the understanding of all.

Forming an Interpretation: Monitor Your Own Thinking

REFLECTION QUESTIONS FOR ELICITING AND PROBING

As you elicit and probe student thinking, reflect on the following questions to help you interpret where students are right now:

- What do students understand?
- What do students misunderstand?
- What are students trying?
- Are students working together equitably?
- How are students representing their thinking (on paper, symbolically, or with manipulatives)? How does this match what they are saying?
- What do they seem to be struggling with? ▪

Eliciting and probing go hand in hand with interpreting. As you ask questions of students, you are thinking carefully about what they say. In listening to their responses and looking at their physical work, you should be looking for the understandings and misunderstandings that are guiding how they have constructed their work. You'll want to pay attention to the nature of the collaboration and determine how equitable it is. You'll want to examine their representations to see how they connect with or differ from what students are saying about their work. And you'll want to look for areas of struggle. If the task is just right, it will induce some productive struggle and knowing where, how, and with what students are struggling is part of interpreting their work. Some guiding reflection questions are provided in the box for you to think about as you elicit and probe students' thinking.

Interpreting what students understand and misunderstand, what they are struggling with or trying, and how they are working together is challenging work that necessarily evolves across the conversation. When you approach students at work, you may begin to form a tentative interpretation before you even ask the first question. As you scan the body language, tone, and physical state of the work, you may get an idea of how students are working. Eliciting and probing help you gather more data and test your developing theories. Let's look at how interpreting evolves during eliciting and probing and helps shape the questions you might ask.

In Cindy's third-grade classroom, the students were working on solving the following open-ended task:

> There are 8 tables in our classroom. I put the same number of markers on each table. How many markers might I need altogether?

Cindy's goal was to push her students to think in equal groups and connect skip counting, equal groups, and different representations to multiplication. As she approached Foa and Jonathan to confer, she noticed that they were both huddled around a single piece of paper and Foa was holding the pencil. Cindy could see Foa's pencil moving and Jonathan appeared to be watching, but she couldn't hear any talk. Cindy sat down next to the pair and watched for a moment, at which time she could hear that Foa was counting under her breath.

Even before Cindy started conferring, she began to form an interpretation, though she began with wonders. She wondered if the work was shared, because Foa appeared to be in control of the pencil and the counting. She wondered what strategy they were using to approach the equal groups problem, noting that they were not using manipulatives. She also interpreted that they were trying something related to the task and that either Foa or both Foa and Jonathan had an idea that involved counting. Cindy began with a general eliciting question.

CINDY: What are you guys trying?

FOA: We're doing 7.

CINDY: 7 what? Say more.

FOA: 7 markers. On the tables.

At this point, Cindy already begins to refine her interpretation. First, she notices that Foa has chosen a number of markers to put on the tables, which fits the parameters of the open-ended task. Foa has been the only speaker, and this reinforces Cindy's question about the access Jonathan has to the work. She decides to ask a specific eliciting question about the pair's next step, but to direct it at Jonathan to see whether he understands the work Foa recorded.

CINDY: So, Jonathan, after you guys decided to put 7 markers on each table, what did you do?

JONATHAN: Foa drew a picture.

CINDY: What does the picture show? Here, can we put the paper in the middle so we can all see? Jonathan, tell me about this picture.

Cindy looks at the picture and sees something unexpected. Rather than circles with lines inside, which some other groups have drawn to show tables with markers on them, Foa has drawn a picture with lines in a row and dots on top.

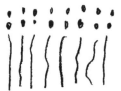

Cindy notices 8 lines with 2 dots on top of each. She wonders how this represents the task of placing markers on 8 tables and the choice Foa and Jonathan have made to use 7 markers.

JONATHAN: We did 7 markers.

CINDY: Where are the markers?

JONATHAN: (*Points at each column of dots and a line.*) 7 markers, 7 markers, 7, 7, 7 . . .

Cindy doesn't see how these dots and a line are 7 markers but hears that this is what Jonathan says. Cindy shifts her questions away from wondering whether this partnership is equitable. Jonathan is trying to answer her questions and he appears confident in his answers, even if Cindy doesn't understand them yet. Foa has let him talk and not dominated the conversation. Cindy is now wondering how this drawing represents the task. Because her question "Where are the markers?" didn't make the representation clearer, Cindy decides to ask the pair to show her how they are using it, so she can see how the drawing is working for them, or not.

CINDY: Can you guys show me how you use this to figure out how many markers we need in all?

(*Foa picks up her pencil and moves it across the lines counting softly under her breath.*)

CINDY: Could you count out loud so I can hear how it works?

FOA: (*Touching each line with her pencil.*) 5, 10, 15, 20, 25, 30, 35, 40. (*Foa writes 40 next to the lines. Then she touches the pairs of dots with her pencil.*) 2, 4, 6, 8, 10, 12, 14, 16. (*Foa writes 16 next to the dots.*)

Watching Foa count, Cindy interprets that the lines represent 5 and each dot represents 1. So, taken together, 1 line and 2 dots would make 7. Cindy thinks this is what Jonathan meant when he said the lines and dots were 7 markers, but she wants to check this assumption. Decomposing 7 into 5 and 2 is an unusual approach, but skip counting by twos and fives is certainly far easier than skip counting by sevens. Cindy wants to probe how they decided on this approach, which could be useful in the future.

CINDY: So, I saw you count the lines by fives and then the dots by twos. Is that right?

FOA: Yeah. Fives and twos.

CINDY: Why did you count by fives and then by twos?

FOA: Sevens are hard, so I broke it up. I put five here and two up there to make it faster.

JONATHAN: Yeah.

CINDY: Jonathan, why does that make sense?

JONATHAN: We can count by fives and we can count by twos. It's easier. I know my fives and twos.

Cindy's questions have confirmed that Jonathan and Foa have developed an interesting skip-counting strategy for dealing with a group of difficult size, 7. Their strategy of decomposing 7 into 5 and 2 makes mathematical sense, and the partners both seem to understand this. They have not completed their strategy yet, by composing the 40 and 16, and Cindy will want to ask them what comes next. However, at this stage Cindy has developed an interpretation of their thinking that she feels confident in.

In this vignette, Cindy's interpretation of her students' thinking evolved as she got more information. It is worth noticing how her changing interpretation affected the questions she asked, leading her to investigate different aspects of the work, shifting from the collaboration to their novel representation. Cindy asked lots of targeted eliciting and probing questions to uncover specific features of their work. She asked questions across the partnership to explore her questions about joint work and to promote access for Jonathan. She used a noticing aloud move to draw attention to what she saw Foa do so that they could talk explicitly about her approach to counting. These moves were orchestrated to make what was invisible public while simultaneously supporting Cindy in interpreting what the students understood and were trying.

Forming an interpretation of student thinking is critical to deciding what to do with that thinking. Interpreting takes constant practice, and it is particularly difficult to do on the fly, as it must when conferring. When in doubt of your interpretation, elicit and probe more. If you are unsure, you probably don't have enough information yet. If you get stuck, revoice what you've heard students say and check your understanding. Notice features aloud and ask students to elaborate. Gather more data until you feel confident you can see the task through your students' eyes.

In the next chapter, we will explore what to do with this interpretation. So far, we've used questions to uncover what students have done and how they are making sense in the moment. Next, we consider how to advance that thinking, or nudge, to deepen or extend what students are doing and craft meaningful next steps with them.

COMMON QUESTIONS

How do I decide who to talk to? I can't talk to everyone every day.

You cannot talk to everyone every day, unless you have a very small class and students work in groups of four. Instead, it is a more reasonable goal to aim to talk to every student over two or three days. It can help to keep track of how frequently you have conferred with different students so that you don't go too long without talking to any individual. So, how to decide who to talk to? Some partnerships are likely to be more independent than others. There may be some students you do want to see every day for a while. You should also consider who you talked to yesterday. Are there students you want to follow up with? Are there students you haven't talked to in a few days? These are broad strategies for thinking about your pace for conferring across your class. However, on any given day, you'll want to stand back and watch students head off to work. As they do, observe the class as a whole for collaboration, the work, tone, and organization. If you see students having difficulty getting started or talking loudly as if arguing, that would be a good place to start. Alternatively, if you see students selecting an unexpected manipulative, you may want to give them a chance to try it out and confer with them second. Keeping in mind the value of productive struggle, you do want to intervene when kids are stuck. If you observe students who are clearly stuck, they should be your next conference.

What if I get brief or one-word answers?

Providing lengthy, detailed explanations requires lots of practice. If students are new to being asked about their thinking or lack confidence in the worthiness of their ideas, they may give very short answers to your eliciting questions. To help students learn to describe their thinking, you may want to try a few different strategies. First, lower the stakes a bit by asking a specific, but open question, such as, "What did you do first?" or "Tell me what's happening in the story (or task)." These questions reduce the vast task of describing all of what is going on in their minds to something a bit narrower. This may give some students a way in. Second, you can create a different way to participate in the moment by asking a quiet student's partner an eliciting question and then asking the quiet student to revoice. This move shifts the student's role to actively listening and makes that a legitimate way to participate. Third, you can give the student lots of wait time and simply be patient for the student to add on, say more, or answer your questions. Remember that these questions can be a scaffold for learning to explain, so think of the questions as gently coaching the student on what thinking to share. The more patient you are, the more it shows that you value the student's thinking and find it worth your time. Finally, if you get a brief answer, it could be that you asked the wrong question. Simply try a different question.

What if one student always answers my questions and no one else speaks?

When you observe lopsided participation in conferring, it could indicate that participation was just as inequitable before you arrived. Sometimes one student seizes control over the group's work and makes it hard for others to find a way in. Alternatively, one student might see a clear pathway toward solving the problem and proceed without including others or explaining their ideas. Heterogeneous groups mean that students come to the work with different understandings, and it takes work to bridge and make use of everyone's thinking. Use deliberate moves to elicit and probe across the partnership. Assess what all members understand. Notice aloud that only one member of the group is talking. You might even ask directly whether the work or thinking was shared.

How do I know when I'm done eliciting?

You're done eliciting and probing when you have an interpretation that you've tested through your questions and feel confident in. If you start down the path of nudging, and you feel like it's not going well or that you're losing your way, come back to eliciting. Anytime your interpretation feels shaky or you have doubts, you can always elicit and probe to gather more data and figure out how to proceed.

REFLECTING ON YOUR OWN PRACTICE

As you think about getting started with conferring, the following guiding questions might help you reflect on how you currently interact with students about their work in the moment, how you learn about their thinking, and what you'd like to try next:

- What is your stance when you approach students to confer? Consider audio-recording yourself as you confer with students and listening. What is the tone? What stance do you hear? Is there anything you need to try to move toward a genuinely curious stance?

- What moves do you already use to elicit or probe student thinking? What moves would you like to try out?

- When do you elicit student thinking? How could you create more opportunities to elicit student thinking and make it the center of your work?

- Are your tasks and norms setting you up well to elicit and interpret student thinking? What might you need to revise to have more thinking to talk about?

- When you talk to students about shared work, how are you learning about all students' thinking?
- What are you thinking about when you elicit student thinking? Are you jumping to any conclusions? What kinds of questions do you want to ask to gather more data?

4 **Nudging:** Growing Student Thinking in the Moment

Once we think we understand where students are, how do we advance their thinking? Students could grow in so many ways, and one challenge for us as teachers is to decide what aspect of their work to nudge forward. In my research, I have found that nudges can focus on one of five different pathways, regardless of the grade level or mathematical concepts: conceptual understanding, developing a strategy, representation, communication, or collaboration. Each points students toward considering a different aspect of their work. Our job is to determine which pathway might be the most productive given what students currently understand and what they are jointly grappling with. All the eliciting and probing work we do at the beginning of conferring fuels this decision. These nudges are a critical way to differentiate instruction for your students, so that what you push is tailored to what students need in the moment.

In this chapter we'll take a look at examples of each of these types of nudges, their goals, and when each might be useful to students. Students send signals about what they need, and using a set of guiding questions, we'll examine how to read these signals to decide on the type of nudge mostly likely to be supportive. Then, we'll dig deeper into the moves

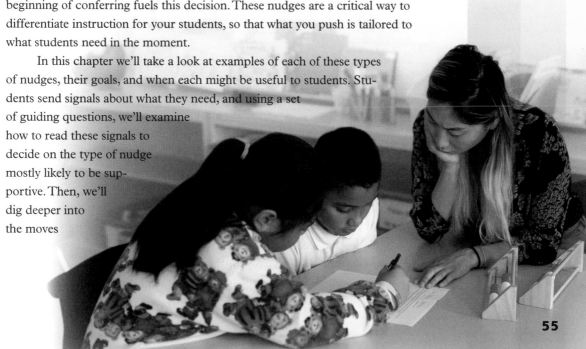

teachers can use to advance student thinking. Some moves can be useful across different types of nudges, and others tend to be more useful for specific types. Finally, we'll look at five vignettes, one for each type of nudge, and highlight the moves teachers used in each.

What Is a Nudge?

Compared with eliciting and probing, nudging often happens fast (in just a few talking turns). It takes time to surface what students are doing and how they understand their work. Once you form a solid interpretation of the state of students' thinking, it is time to nudge. In the space of a few moments, the teacher and the students move from what they have done to something new. The nudge has four critical features:

1. Nudges are initiated by the teacher to advance students' mathematical thinking, engagement in mathematical practice, or collaboration.
2. Nudges are responsive to elicited student thinking.
3. Nudges are taken up by students.
4. Nudges maintains student ownership and sense-making.

Nudges Are a Joint Project

Nudging is not simply something we do *to* students but something we do *with* them. The moves we use depend in large part on what students themselves say back to us. As a teacher, you need to choose a pathway to point your students down, one you believe will support their thinking and help them grow. You need to make a specific move to show them that pathway. This direction is not something wildly new. Rather, it builds on what you've learned about where they are right now through all your eliciting and probing. You might say, "How are you going to include your partners in this work?" if students are struggling to collaborate effectively. This move should be an authentic question, one with many legitimate answers.

Then, you have to stay and listen. It is one thing for you to have an idea for a productive avenue for work and quite another for students to take up your suggestion and make it their own. The first thing to listen for is *uptake*. When you initiate a nudge, like the one in the previous paragraph, you must listen to how students respond to hear whether they are taking up your suggestion. They don't always. They might fall silent, or push back, a phenomenon we will talk more about in Chapter 5. But if your nudge makes sense to students, you will be able to hear that it makes sense in how they respond to your suggestion. Students will need to generate some ideas, reason about what you've suggested, and agree on an idea. This hard work is how we know whether students are making sense of the mathematics and whether the ideas are truly theirs, not ours.

When you hear uptake, you need to listen for *how* students have taken up your suggestion and how they are beginning to make it their own. You cannot know before students open their mouths what it is that you are going to say in return. You must listen to your students, take their responses seriously, and determine how to reply in a way that builds on their thinking. They may need you to ask additional follow-up questions, ask questions that support making connections, or scaffold listening to one another's thinking. Remember that it is a critical sign that students are making the nudge part of their own work when you didn't know precisely what the outcome was going to look like. Nudging is not a cookie-cutter affair, because students are all different thinkers. And if it turns out the nudge wasn't the right one for these kids in this moment, you'll need the opportunity to try again.

Deciding How to Respond: Five Types of Nudges

In the sections that follow, we'll take a close look at each type of nudge, its purpose, and how you know when it's the right choice for your students. At the end of the chapter, each type of nudge is illustrated with a vignette.

Nudges can point students down one of five pathways for advancing their thinking.

1. **CONCEPTUAL UNDERSTANDING:** At the heart of the work, students are grappling with mathematical ideas. These nudges help students to think about the mathematical ideas that underpin the task they are engaged in or to make mathematical meaning of the task. This might look like focusing on place value and the meanings of digits or on interpreting what is happening in a task instead of jumping to doing things with numbers.

2. **DEVELOPING A STRATEGY:** Once students understand what the task is asking, they need to develop a way of tackling it. These nudges support students in generating ideas for a strategy, an approach, or a first step for entering a task based on their mathematical

understandings. For instance, if students accurately interpret a problem as joining two numbers, this nudge might help them think about how they will join those numbers.

3. **REPRESENTATION:** How students represent their thinking, either on paper or with manipulatives, is critical to learning. These nudges prompt students to generate ways of representing their ideas so that others can see them and so that they themselves can grapple with the mathematical practice of modeling. Representation is anything visible that furthers students' thinking about and connection within mathematics, from counting cubes to writing expressions.

4. **COMMUNICATION:** Beyond explaining their thinking to you when you ask eliciting questions, students need to learn how to construct complete, convincing explanations of their work. In your classroom, you may have a variety of venues for this, such as sharing strategies in a whole-class discussion following the work or constructing written explanations to share with parents or peers. These nudges help students to generate ideas for how to fully communicate their reasoning to others.

5. **COLLABORATION:** Beyond the mathematical ideas themselves, collaborative problem-solving requires sophisticated skills for joint work, including explaining, asking questions, listening, and negotiating. Collaborations can be fraught with issues of power and authority that make working together more challenging. These nudges help students negotiate this tricky terrain so that they can proceed with mathematical thinking together, without anyone being left out.

The Conceptual Understanding Nudge

A central purpose of engaging students in challenging mathematical tasks is to support them in developing conceptual understanding. We want students to know more than procedures. We want them to know how and why things work; we want them to make sense. Nudges that focus on conceptual understanding draw students' attention to the mathematical ideas that underpin the task they are working on and prompt them to make meaning of these ideas. To see a conceptual understanding nudge unfold, read the vignettes starting on page 71.

How do you know when to nudge conceptual understanding?

Some signals that students could use a nudge on conceptual understanding include:

- Students express confusion about the task, what it's asking, or what is happening.
- Students tell you about a procedure they used but cannot justify it why it works when you probe.
- Eliciting surfaces a mathematical misconception.
- Students seem to be guessing about what to do, perhaps by just picking an operation.
- Students struggle to answer questions probing for reasoning.

Each of these signs indicates that students may be struggling with or missing a key mathematical concept inherent in the task. This may well be why you chose this task as the work for the day, so that it would challenge students to grapple with a worthy concept. A conceptual understanding nudge will allow you to focus on addressing misconceptions, deepening reasoning, and interpreting tasks.

CONCEPTUAL UNDERSTANDING NUDGE

4.1   Faith's second graders were working on the following task:

> **My mom has 20 packs of 10 Halloween pencils and 4 loose ones. How many Halloween pencils does she have? How do you know?**

In this conference, Faith's students were confused about the mathematical meaning of the task and wanted to represent the total number of pencils as 20 + 4. Although the students had experience with thinking in tens and ones, they had never grappled with so many tens in a task. Faith nudges them on the meaning of 20 in this task and what a "pack of 10 pencils" looks like, connecting the mathematics to the context of the story. Notice that Faith does not stay to guide them through the task but instead supports them in making meaning so they can get going.

The Develop a Strategy Nudge

Nudges focused on supporting students to develop a strategy are perhaps the most straightforward to understand. Once students understand what the task is asking them, they need a solution pathway. Students need opportunities to construct their own solution pathways by developing strategies that make sense to them. The strategies students invent do not have to (and typically don't) mirror conventional methods; the only important criteria are that the strategies are grounded in mathematics, make sense to the student who is using them, and evolve over time. This nudge supports students in all three of these criteria by focusing on sense-making, maintaining students' choice, and identifying opportunities for students to refine their strategies over time. To see a develop a strategy nudge unfold, read the vignettes starting on page 74.

How do you know when to nudge students to develop a strategy?
Some signals that students could use a nudge to develop a strategy include:

- Students understand the task but have not yet figured out a strategy for solving.
- Students are trying a strategy but are frustrated or not satisfied with how it's working.
- Students are using the same inefficient or labor-intensive strategy they have been using for a long time.

Each of these signs indicates that students may be struggling with developing solution pathways that make sense and are continuing to evolve. Inventing strategies to solve problems is not something students do once. Rather, strategies are constantly growing and refining, and students benefit from support in this long-term process. As teachers we hope students will be engaged in this work of developing new strategies, testing them on different kinds of tasks, finding ways to make them more accurate, and noticing patterns that lead to efficiency. Developing a strategy nudges make space for you to support this process as it unfolds for each student.

DEVELOP A STRATEGY NUDGE

 4.2 Mary wanted to push her student to think about the meaning of the traditional algorithm for subtraction, which they had learned in previous years, and to struggle with larger numbers when she offered her students some work produced by a fictional student the class named Jeffy. Jeffy had used this method to subtract 1,707 − 550 and he had gotten 1,257 as the result. The students are asked to figure out if Jeffy's work was correct and justify their decision. In the conference in this clip, Mary first elicits the students' thinking about what the task is and finds that the two partners disagree about whether Jeffy's work is accurate. Notice the moves that Mary uses to elicit and probe across the partnership and how she supports the students in connecting different strategies to make sense out of the subtraction. Note that Mary closes the conference when it is clear that the students have a plan, rather than walking through that plan with them step by step.

The Representation Nudge

Representation nudges focus on how students show their thinking with manipulatives, numbers, words, drawings, symbols, graphs, tables, or any other visible documentation. When students have mathematical ideas about the task and about how they might solve it, they need ways to record their thinking. It is important to note that recording thinking is more than "show your work." There are several purposes for mathematical representation that are far more important than proving to your teacher that you did it. First, mathematicians need to keep track of their thinking, particularly when there are several steps, the numbers get too large to hold in one's head, or there are many parts. Writing things down so they are clearly labeled helps students to keep track of their thinking and ensure accuracy. Second, representation itself can allow students to use their thinking by revealing patterns or making strategies generalizable to other tasks. Finally, representation allows others the opportunity to understand—and be convinced by—a person's thinking. At the close of mathematical work each day, when students have an opportunity to share their thinking, the representations they have made give others access and support discussion. To see a representation nudge unfold, read the vignette starting on page 77.

How do you know when to nudge representation?

Some signals that students could use a nudge on representation include:

- Students provide an oral description of their thinking, strategy, or solution but have little or none of that thinking captured on paper or with objects.
- Students find it difficult to explain their thinking clearly orally, and a picture, diagram, or other representation would make their ideas clearer.
- Students solve the task fluently mentally, but their thinking might be difficult for other students to follow.
- Students can show their thinking with fingers or objects but do not yet have a way to keep their thinking for later use.
- Specific forms of representation are a focus of the current mathematical work, such as using symbols or making a graph.

These conditions indicate that students are ready to think about how to take their ideas and make them visible and accessible to others. Representation nudges will give students the support to consider how to layer on representations by adding numbers to pictures or adding number sentences to label the action symbolically. Sometimes this representation may even be the focus of the work you've asked students to do, in which case the representation nudges provide an opportunity to encourage students to take up and use those mathematical structures in their work.

> **REPRESENTATION NUDGE**
>
> **4.3** Faith's second graders were counting collections of objects by organizing them in groups of 10 to deepen their understanding of place value. The students Faith confers with in this clip have organized a large collection of blocks into many groups of 10. Faith asks them to count these orally, and they confront what happens after 190. Faith nudges the students to figure out how they might represent the quantity with number names and numerals and how these two representations are related to place value.

The Communication Nudge

Students need to be able to talk about their thinking in ways that are sequenced, logical, complete, precise, and convincing. This is a lot to ask of anyone in the midst of learning. Students need opportunities to learn how to articulate their processes and then name their ideas using mathematical language so that others can follow and understand them. When we elicit student thinking, we are often getting "first-draft" explanations, and like any first draft they need revision. Communication nudges create space for students to work on this revision so that they can share their thinking with an audience. Communication nudges are related to and sometimes overlap with representation nudges. Both create opportunities for students to make their thinking public in ways that are clear and convincing. Although representation nudges focus on showing thinking and tap into the mathematical practice of modeling and reasoning abstractly, communication nudges focus on language to promote explanation, justification, and argumentation. To see a communication nudge unfold, read the vignette starting on page 78.

How do you know when to nudge communication?

Some signals that students could use a nudge on communication include:

- Students have mathematical thinking you want them to be able to share with others.
- Students provide an explanation with potential that is either incomplete or out of sequence.
- Students are convinced of their own thinking but struggle to explain it.
- Additional writing would make students' representation more convincing.

In each of these situations, students have already done mathematical work grounded in sense-making and may have followed a solution pathway to an answer, but they would benefit from an opportunity to work on how they explain that work before sharing with others or writing about their thinking. Communication nudges allow you to create space for a second or third oral draft of students' explanations, as you press on areas than need clarification, precision, or elaboration. If your aim is to support students in writing a complete and convincing explanation, then these oral rehearsals can be explicitly named as talking about what students will then write.

COMMUNICATION NUDGE

4.4 This conference took place on the same day as the one shown in Clip 4.1, during which the second graders were asked to figure out how many pencils Faith's mom had when she bought 20 packs of 10 and 4 loose ones. These students had first modeled this task as 2 sticks of 10 cubes and 4 extra cubes but then figured out how to model it as 20 sticks of 10 cubes and 4 extra cubes. Faith nudges them to rehearse how to explain why they changed their mind to the whole class during the discussion.

The Collaboration Nudge

Collaborative problem-solving is about both the problem-solving and the collaboration. Students are learning both how mathematics works and how to work together. As teachers, we need to explicitly teach students what engaging in mathematics together looks like and sounds like. Even with this instruction, partnerships sometimes stumble or break down. Challenges in collaboration often stem from one of two sources: skills and status. At times students lack the skill to negotiate ideas, listen to and consider the thinking of others, or ask questions to clarify meaning. Alternatively, students may deliberately exclude one or more members of a group because they are viewed as having lower status. Exclusion devalues the contributions of others and can make the excluded student appear off task. Collaboration nudges provide support for students to learn how to work together equitably. To see a collaboration nudge unfold, read the vignettes starting on page 80.

How do you know when to nudge collaboration?

Some signals that students could use a nudge on collaboration include:

- Students are working in parallel on different strategies.
- Partners are arguing about taking turns, the use of manipulatives, or who gets to write.
- One or more partners are excluded from the work.
- All of the mathematical work, such as the paper, pencil, and tools, are controlled by one student.
- Only one partner can explain the work happening.

Note that some of these signs can be seen from afar. Pay attention to the distribution of materials and students' body language. When you approach students at work, listen to how they interact, whose ideas matter, and whether anyone is issuing commands or being ignored. When you elicit thinking, if there is a dramatic asymmetry of responses or arguments ensue, you'll want to attend to the way collaboration is functioning for these students. A collaboration nudge will support students in launching productively into joint work.

Deciding Which Nudge to Use

Figure 4.1 is a quick reference tool that includes guiding questions you can ask yourself to help determine which nudge to use.

Whatever type of nudge we decide on, we don't control what students say, we cannot fully predict their responses, and we cannot pull teeth to get them to do something we want them to. Instead, we have to work with our students to construct a nudge together. Let's take a look at some of the moves that can lead to productive nudges.

Guiding Questions for Deciding What Kind of Nudge Students Need

Are you noticing . . .	Then you might want to nudge . . .
Students not yet understanding the task? Misconceptions? Struggle with mathematical ideas?	Conceptual understanding
Students understand the task but don't know how to get started? Students trying something but getting stuck? Frustration with the strategy students are trying?	Developing a strategy
Students can explain their thinking but have little or nothing recorded? Students stumbling as they explain because their idea is difficult to describe with words alone?	Representation
An idea that you would like to see shared with the class clearly? An accurate, but inefficient, imprecise, or unclear explanation of mathematical thinking? A written representation that would be clearer or more precise with writing?	Communication
A student being excluded? Unequal distribution of materials, work, or talk? Arguments about turns, materials, or decisions? Parallel work, rather that joint work?	Collaboration

FIGURE 4.1

Moves That Support Nudging: What Do I Say?

The moves used in nudging need to be flexible to adapt to the myriad moments you will encounter with students. At times you will need to support intellectual risk-taking, help students listen to one another, clarify misconceptions, or facilitate the development of an actionable plan. As you learn to nudge your students, you'll need to improvise moves that support students, and you may find yourself inventing new ways of nudging—no list of moves can ever account for every situation. But to get you started, we'll look at a set of moves that can be useful for different kinds of nudges. For each move, you'll find a description of the move, some examples of what it can sound like, and the type of nudge it is most often used to support. Later in the chapter, you'll see what they look like in the context of the five types of nudges.

Noticing Aloud and Asking

Noticing aloud is stating something specific that you noticed students said, wrote, or did that you want to focus attention on. Then, you can ask a question that gets students to reason or generate ideas about that narrow slice of their work. Use this move to focus discussion on a specific aspect of students' thinking, such as a misconception, inconsistency, or missing part, or something that you want them to reason about or extend. This move is naturally very tailored to the moment and what students are doing. The following are a few examples of what it could sound like in different situations:

- I notice that one of you said it was 4 and one of you said it was 4 tens. Which is it?
- You just explained your thinking so clearly, but I notice that your paper is blank. How can you show what you just said?
- I notice that your partner can't see the paper. How can you sit so everyone can participate?

USE IT TO NUDGE: Any type

Specifying

Specifying involves asking follow-up questions that make students' plan or idea more specific and actionable. Use it when students state a general idea about what they are going to do, but greater detail is needed for them to act, or the specific details make a difference and you want to support students in making decisions. For instance, students might say they want to "use a number line" to solve a problem, which is mathematically appropriate, but *how* they will use it matters. Specifying moves push students to think through the details, which might need to be negotiated between partners, before you leave them to enact their plan. These moves are tailored to the specific situation, as you follow up on students' ideas. The following are some additional examples of how specifying can sound:

- What are you going to do with the ruler? How will you use it?
- How will you set up the table? What columns will you need?
- So, you are going to share. What is everyone's job going to be? How will you take turns?
- What will you add? Why does that make sense?

USE IT TO NUDGE: Any type

Retelling

Retelling is used to help students articulate and visualize the mathematical task, so they can find a way to enter it. In this move you ask students to tell, in their own words, what the task or story is, so that it makes sense and is clear to all. Students in a group can construct these retellings together and act out parts of the story. Often students have trouble getting started simply because they get lost in the words. Retelling gives them a foothold in imagining the mathematical situation. You might say:

- Let's go back to the story. What's happening in the story?
- Who can retell?
- What's this task about? Explain it to me.
- Then what happened?
- What does that look like? Can we act it out?
- What does it mean when it says _____ in the story?

USE IT TO NUDGE: Conceptual understanding

Orienting to Partners

Moves that orient students to their partners can take two forms. First, these moves can simply be you, as the teacher, deliberately soliciting the thinking, opinions, and ideas of all students. One student may take the lead in speaking for the group, but this undermines collaboration and can mask inequity. By intentionally asking others, you enrich the ideas of the group, build agreement, and model equitable discourse. Second, these moves can prompt students to engage with one another's thinking by asking them to revoice what someone else has said, offer agreement or disagreement with reasoning, or respond directly to their partner, rather than talking through the teacher (Chapin, O'Connor, and Anderson 2013). These moves can sound like:

- Marco, do you agree or disagree with what Kini just said? Why?
- Justin, what do you think?
- Does anyone want to add on to what she just said?
- Rebecca, I notice I haven't heard from you yet. What are you thinking about?
- What did you just hear your partner say? Can you revoice?

- You can ask him to repeat what he just said if you didn't hear him.
- Tell your partner what you're thinking.

USE IT TO NUDGE: Any, but especially collaboration

Positioning Students with Competence

Moves that position students with competence have been shown to broaden and deepen participation by supporting students' identities as competent doers of math (Cohen and Lotan 2014; Featherstone et al. 2011). Positioning students with competence means taking their ideas seriously, expressing confidence in their developing thinking, and elevating their status within their group if inequities exist. These moves are particularly important when confidence is low, risk-taking is fragile, or a student in the group is viewed as not having worthy ideas. Positioning students with competence can involve explicitly saying that an idea has value and should be considered. It can involve naming concrete accomplishments or noticing efforts before asking students to elaborate or move forward (Munson 2018). The following are a few examples of how this might sound:

- You have an idea. What is it?
- I see you thinking hard. What are you thinking about?
- Rohit just said something really important. What are you going to ask him about his idea?
- You've told me about the drawing you made and how it represents the story. I see the apples and the pies. How can you use your drawing to help you?

USE IT TO NUDGE: Any

The Could Move: Generating Possibilities

The could move is one of my favorites because it is so flexible and opens up a brainstorming space where risks are much easier to take. It simply involves framing your questions with the word *could* to encourage students to think about possibilities, rather than what they *should* do (Munson 2018). Use it to shift students from trying to remember what they are supposed to do to thinking creatively about what they might try. This move focuses students on coming up with ideas before they turn one of them into a plan, creating space to think before deciding. The could move can sound like:

- What could you do?
- What could it look like?
- How could you explain it?
- What could you try?
- How could you show your thinking?
- What materials could you use?

USE IT TO NUDGE: Any, but especially developing a strategy

Making Connections

A central part of inquiry is discovering how ideas are connected and creating a mental map of an ever-evolving network of mathematical concepts. Making connections moves prompt students to connect ideas, tasks, stories, manipulatives, numbers, drawings, graphs, tables, patterns, and words so that no idea is ever isolated, but rather everything makes sense in the broader context of mathematics. Use these moves to prompt students to consider how ideas and representations are related, how they show the same thing, are similar, or are different. Within a particular mathematical task, students may be thinking using numbers, manipulatives, drawings, words, and symbols, and all should be related in ways that are meaningful to the students who use them. Making connections moves highlight these relationships and may reveal useful, generalizable patterns. These moves can sound like:

- How is the number sentence connected to the story?
- How is your strategy related to the strategy your partner just shared?
- I see you used tens and ones to add on your paper. Where are those tens and ones on the rekenrek (or base ten blocks)?
- How does this drawing show what's happening in the story?
- How does this graph show the data in the table?
- You just said _____. Where is that in your picture?
- How is what you did in this problem like what you did in the last problem?

USE IT TO NUDGE: Conceptual understanding, developing a strategy, communication, or representation

Orienting Students to an Audience

Orienting students to an audience involves making clear with whom, how, and why students' thinking will be shared (Engle et al. 2012). Sometimes students push back on our suggestions that they write, represent, or explain thinking because they believe that the answer is what matters. Giving students an authentic audience can create a need for the very writing, representation, and explanation that you value. All the work students do to invent and struggle with ideas needs to have a venue. That includes spaces for students to discuss questions, struggles, and mistakes, as well as opportunities to share new discoveries, patterns, and strategies so that others can learn from them. Knowing that there are audiences for work motivates students to make their work clear, organized, and easy to follow. This move is typically included as a reason within other moves, such as:

- How could you represent that so that others can see what you're thinking?
- During the discussion, I'm going to ask you to share what you did. How can you explain it to the class so that they will understand?
- How could you show your thinking so that when I put it up in the hallway all the parents understand what you just told me?
- I think I understand what you're thinking, but I can see your partner is confused. How could you explain your plan so that your partner can understand?

USE IT TO NUDGE: Representation and communication

Prompting Immediate Action

At times students share ideas for what they might do but seem to be waiting to take action. Sometimes they lack confidence, or they may seem to be pondering the idea. Moves that prompt immediate action communicate to students that there is no need to wait. This move expresses that trying ideas is how we learn and that it is important to dive in to see what will happen. We do not need to wait for perfection to proceed. If an idea doesn't work, then we'll know and can come up with another idea. Use this to move kids from dwelling or hesitating to action. This move sounds like:

- Great. Let's do it.
- Let's give it a try. Who's going to go get the ruler?
- Let's see how it goes. What do we need to get started?

USE IT TO NUDGE: Any

Closing a Conference

Every conference needs closure, and there are several productive ways to do so. Three closings that are portable to many conferences are: encouraging students to try their ideas, crystallizing the mathematical point, and prompting reflection. Let's look at each in turn.

A nudge should accomplish something. It could support students in understanding something new, creating a pathway through a problem, generating ideas for showing work or explaining thinking, or repairing a damaged partnership. At the end, if students have come up with a clear next step, one useful way to close the conference is to encourage students to try their new ideas. This might sound like:

- Try it. I'm curious what you discover.
- Give that a try! I'll be back to see how it's going.
- I can't wait to see what you find!

Alternatively, if students have arrived at some new thinking or an important idea surfaced in the interaction, you might close the conference by crystallizing the mathematical point of the conversation. This closing is particularly useful when there is an idea that you want the students to hold onto for use in the future. The way these closings sound is specific to the mathematics you've discussed. For instance, it could sound like:

- The rekenrek helped you to think in tens and ones. So anytime you want to work with tens and ones, the rekenrek is a useful tool.
- Your idea of using a table let you see new patterns. Next time you're looking for patterns, ask yourself if a table might help.
- You asked an important question—will this always work? When you think you've found a strategy, this is a great question to ask yourself!

Finally, you might want to close by offering students the opportunity to reflect on their work or thinking. This kind of closing encourages metacognition and can be powerful when you confer at the end of working on a task. After students have finished, reflection about the process can help them to consider what made sense and what choices they would make in solving future problems. Becoming aware of their own thinking equips students to make thoughtful, sense-driven choices. This could sound like:

- You solved this problem in two ways. Which strategy made the most sense to you? Why?

- What helped you to figure out what this task was asking?
- Why do you think this tool worked better for you?

The moves discussed in this section are not an exhaustive list. Rather, this is the beginning of a tool kit that you can add to and refine over time as you respond to your own students. In the vignettes in the following section, you may notice additional moves you'd like to try as you confer.

What Nudges Sound Like: Five Vignettes

Each nudge type sounds a little different, in ways that match their different goals. If you've watched the video examples earlier in the chapter, you've had a glimpse at how different nudges can sound. In this section, we take a slower look at each nudge and examine how teachers use moves in concert to nudge students' thinking forward along each of the five avenues.

As you read each vignette, you'll notice that moves of different types are highlighted and annotated at the side to give you a chance to see how they come to life in conferring. These questions can help students talk about their changing thinking as it happens. You'll notice a few things as you read the annotated dialogue. First, sometimes teachers use eliciting and probing questions as part of nudging, too. Second, teachers often repeat the same kinds of moves more than once in a nudge, and some types of moves are more frequent in certain types of nudges. Finally, some moves are doing more than one job; for instance, a move can be both a notice aloud and ask and a could move at the same time. Let's take a look at each type of nudge in turn.

What Conceptual Understanding Nudges Sound Like

Conceptual understanding nudges can take two forms. First, they might focus on the task itself. What does the task mean? What is happening in the task? Sometimes students cannot get started simply because they are struggling to make mathematical meaning of the task. Second, they can draw attention to a mathematical idea that is posing a challenge and give students a chance to construct meaning. We'll look at examples of each, starting with focusing on the meaning of the task.

In Anne's fourth-grade classroom the students were engaged in a fractions task. On the previous day the students had figured out that if a submarine sandwich was going to be shared equally between 5 friends, each friend would get $\frac{1}{5}$ of the sandwich. Today, Anne changed the story, saying that one of the friends, Marco, gave his piece of the sandwich to another friend, Tita, who now has 2 pieces. Anne asked students to figure out what fraction of the sandwich Tita had now. When Anne approached a pair of her students to confer, she noticed that they were not actively working. Anne asked questions about what they were up to and they gave vague answers, like, "We're trying to figure it out." Anne asked what they were trying to figure out and their answers remained general, "The story." Here is how Anne nudged:

Retelling — **ANNE:** So, what is happening in this story? Tell me the story again.

DANIELA: Marco had to leave.

Retelling — **ANNE:** Start at the beginning. Where are we? Who's there?

MATEO: The 5 friends. They're all at the sandwich shop.

DANIELA: Yeah, and each one has a piece.

Specifying — **ANNE:** A piece of what?

DANIELA: Of the sandwich.

Specifying — **ANNE:** How big are their pieces?

MATEO: Each one has $\frac{1}{5}$.

Retelling — **ANNE:** Then what happens?

DANIELA: Marco has to leave.

ANNE: So, what happens when Marco leaves? This is important to the story, right?

(*Mateo and Daniela pause.*)

Retelling — **ANNE:** Let's go back to the story and see what it can tell us.

(*Anne has the students go back to the chart where the task was written for the class to see. After they have read, she asks her question again: What happens when Marco leaves?*)

DANIELA: Oh! He gives it to Tita.

MATEO: Yeah, she has 2 now!

ANNE: So, what do we need to figure out?

MATEO: How much does she have!

Mateo and Daniela start talking about what they could do next. Mateo starts to draw and Daniela leans over giving him her ideas. In this example, Anne identified that her students were struggling to enter and make sense of the task because they didn't understand the action of the story and the question being asked. By asking them to retell the story, she pinpointed where their understanding had broken down, and then she prompted them to go find the information they needed to construct understanding of the task. Notice that this kind of nudge isn't short. It requires a lot of teacher moves to support students in sequencing their understanding and then identifying a specific place where a repair is needed to move forward.

The second form of conceptual understanding nudge can serve to highlight mathematical ideas, so students can reason about them. Here we focus on asking about the meaning of specific ideas, helping students sort out misconceptions, or resolving conflicting ideas.

Anne approached another pair of students who told her a lot about the model they had constructed. On their paper, they had drawn a submarine sandwich, cut into 5 equal pieces. They had labeled each piece with a different friend's name, and then crossed out Marco's name and drawn an arrow to Tita to show giving the piece to her. When Anne posed the question from the task—How much does Tita get?—the students were confused. James thought it was 2 and $\frac{1}{5}$, while Tupa disagreed but didn't have another way to name the amount. These students understood the task but were struggling with how fractions relate to quantity. Here is how Anne nudged:

ANNE: So, I notice, Tupa, that you're not convinced. I'm wondering what each of these pieces means. I see that you've labeled each one with the person's name, so it's really clear which pieces belong to Tita. But how much is each piece?   — *Noticing Aloud and Asking*

TUPA: A fifth, each one is a fifth.

ANNE: James, do you agree or disagree?   — *Orienting to Partners*

JAMES: I agree. We did this yesterday. Each piece is $\frac{1}{5}$.

ANNE: So, how much is it if Tita's got 2 of these $\frac{1}{5}$ pieces?

JAMES: She's got 2 one-fifths.

ANNE: Oh, so that's different than what I thought I heard you say.

TUPA: Yeah, I thought you said 2 *and* $\frac{1}{5}$. That's too much.

ANNE: Why would that be too much? Two *and* $\frac{1}{5}$?   — *Probing*

TUPA: 'Cause that's like 2 whole big sandwiches, and then a piece. But there's only 1 sandwich.

Orienting to Partners ——⎰ **ANNE:** What do you think about that, James?

JAMES: Yeah, not 2 whole sandwiches. Two PIECES, 2 one-fifth.

Probing and Making Connections ——⎰ **ANNE:** Why does 2 one-fifths make sense in this story?

TUPA: 'Cause each piece is $\frac{1}{5}$ and she's got 2 pieces. 2 one-fifths.

JAMES: Yeah, 2 one-fifth pieces.

Tupa starts to write on their paper. In this example, Anne draws the students' attention to their area of mathematical struggle and focuses the conversation on making sense of how we describe multiple unit fractions mathematically. It is worth noting that Tupa and James do not arrive at a conventional answer, but the fraction name they come to agree on makes mathematical sense. The nudge has allowed them to distinguish between two iterations of $\frac{1}{5}$ and $2 + \frac{1}{5}$, and Anne's questions supported Tupa in articulating why he disagreed with James' initial idea. In this way, Anne's conceptual understanding nudge also supported their collaboration by bringing them into agreement about the underlying mathematical ideas.

The conceptual understanding nudge often takes a lot of teacher moves to focus students' attention on the mathematically important details of the work at the point where understanding is breaking down or thin.

What Nudges to Develop a Strategy Sound Like

This nudge supports students in developing new strategies, selecting an appropriate strategy, refining a strategy for greater efficiency or precision, or thinking about how to apply a strategy used in a previous task. Let's first look at an example of students who need to figure what their strategy could be, and then we'll look at how to nudge students to refine or grow a strategic approach.

Grace's first-grade students had been working on counting large collections of classroom objects to build understanding of counting, grouping, and place value. When she approached Matias and Jocelyn to confer, they were working to count a bucket of markers. They had dumped the bucket out onto their table, and markers rolled everywhere. Grace asked them some questions about their plan but kept getting interrupted by their frustration with the markers rolling off the table and onto the floor. Jocelyn said that they had done this with other buckets before. When they counted the cubes and a bin of picture books, they started by emptying the bin, but with the markers it wasn't working. Here is how Grace nudged:

GRACE: So, what you're saying is that with the markers, dumping them on the table first just isn't working. What else could you do to get started with counting so that that markers don't roll away from you?

The Could Move

JOCELYN: Well, we could . . .

MATIAS: We could get another bucket.

GRACE: What could you do with another bucket?

The Could Move and Specifying

MATIAS: Move the markers when we count. You know, like, we could leave them all in here (*pointing to the original bucket*) and then put them in another—.

JOCELYN: Yeah, when we count them. We can put them in the other bucket when we count.

MATIAS: So they won't roll around.

GRACE: Why don't you try that, and I'll come back to see how it's going.

Closing: Encouraging Students to Try Their Ideas

Jocelyn and Matias were struggling with how to effectively organize for counting. This is more than a matter of getting materials; rolling markers lead to inaccurate counting. In fact, the students' frustration was a potent clue to exactly what they needed: a nudge that supported them in developing a strategy that addressed the source of their dissatisfaction and moved them toward counting accurately and systematically. Grace's moves were about focusing the students' attention on the specific challenge they faced and opening space for them to consider how they could navigate it. The students themselves generated the solution pathway, and Grace only asked them to elaborate on what they would do. By the time Grace closed conferring, the students had an idea that was their own and that they could proceed without Grace's support.

When Grace sat down with Jessinia and Joanna across the room, she learned that they had organized paper clips into chains of 5. After Grace asked how they were going to use their groups to help them count, Joanna pointed to the first group and counted 1, 2, 3, 4, 5, then to the second group, 6, 7, 8, 9, 10. Here is how Grace nudged:

Noticing Aloud and Asking

GRACE: I notice that you've connected your paper clips in groups of 5.

JOANNA: Yeah, fives. They're all fives.

GRACE: I noticed when you were counting them you counted 1, 2, 3, 4, 5. You counted each one. I'm wondering if there is a way to use the groups you've made to make counting easier.

JESSINIA: We could count by fives?

Specifying

GRACE: What would that look like?

(Jessinia lays her hand across each string of paper clips as she counts slowly.)

JESSINIA: 5 . . . 10 . . . 15 . . . 20 . . .

Orienting to Partners

GRACE: Joanna, what do you think about this way of counting?

JOANNA: Yeah, that works! You can count by fives. Each one is five.

Closing: Encouraging Students to Try Their Ideas

GRACE: OK, try it. I'm curious what you find.

Jessinia and Joanna already had a well-developed strategy that was organized and could lead to an accurate count. Grace's nudge aimed to refine the strategy so that it was more efficient and used the structures they had already developed. Moving from counting by ones to skip counting is an important step in organizing for counting and ultimately thinking about place value and our number system. These students were poised to move toward counting in groups, and Grace encouraged them to think about how they could.

Notice that developing a strategy nudges are primarily structured to draw students' attention to a strategic problem and ask them to generate ideas for how they could move forward. This is a brainstorming space, and as teachers we guide students to create ideas and grow one or more into a plan. The plan does not need to be complete or efficient (yet). Instead, these nudges help students to develop their strategic thinking from wherever it is. If students have no plan, then this nudge helps them come up with an idea. If students have a plan, then this nudge might help them to make the plan more efficient or accurate. It is also worth noting that you don't need to stay to watch them fully implement the plan and complete the task by arriving at an answer; creating a plan for how to move forward is enough to allow the students to make meaningful progress while the teacher moves on to confer with others.

What Representation Nudges Sound Like

Nudges focused on representation prompt students to develop ways to make their thinking visible. They tend to start with variations on the question, how could you show your thinking? This is often followed by supporting questions that help students think through their representations so that they make sense and accurately represent what students are thinking or what they have done. The nudge that opened this book in Chapter 1 (see page 3) was a representation nudge. In that nudge, the teacher asked students how they could show on paper the strategy they had just described orally. Let's look at another variation on this nudge, in which students move from using fingers to recording with drawings and numbers.

Rafa had asked his first graders to work on solving a problem that involved taking away from a number larger than 10. He knew this was going to pose a challenge because many students used their fingers to solve such problems. He asked, "If 11 students were sitting on the carpet and 2 students left to go to the bathroom, how many students are still on the carpet?" When he approached Dreshon and Adriana, they had put their hands together to help them model the action of the story. They showed Rafa how Dreshon had held up all his fingers and Adriana gave him 1 more, and then if Adriana put 1 finger down and Dreshon put 1 down, there were 9 left. Rafa nudges them to find a way to capture this thinking:

RAFA: I notice that when you guys put your fingers together, it helped you to see how many kids were left on the carpet. But when you put your hands down, we can't see your thinking anymore. Is there a way you could write or show what you did on paper, so we don't lose your thinking?

Noticing Aloud and Asking and the Could Move

ADRIANA: You mean like, draw our hands?

RAFA: You could draw hands. Or you could do something else. What do you think makes sense to show what you did?

Positioning Students with Competence

DRESHON: Draw hands. Yeah, we can do that.

RAFA: What could that look like?

The Could Move and Specifying

ADRIANA *(to Dreshon)*: Put your hands down here so I can trace them. And then you can do my one.

(Dreshon and Adriana trace 2 hands and 1 finger.)

RAFA: So how can you use your picture to show how you figured out how many kids were left on the carpet?

Specifying and Making Connections

ADRIANA: We can put numbers on them and then cross out the 2 fingers.

DRESHON: Yeah, so there's 9 left.

These students had an effective strategy, and by adding representations to their work, Rafa moves them closer to thinking more abstractly and generally about what they have done. In the future, he might ask them to label this kind of representation with another one, a number sentence, making connections between the story, fingers, drawings, numbers, and symbols. Notice that the form of the representation comes from the students, and Rafa's questions focus on how it could look and how they will use it to show their thinking.

These nudges get at the mathematical practice of modeling and the creation of multiple representations, all of which forge important mathematical connections that make students more flexible thinkers. Representation nudges might go beyond simply asking students to represent by articulating why making thinking visible is useful. For instance, teachers might name an audience for the representation by saying, "How could you represent your thinking so that other groups can understand what you did?" Or the teacher could indicate what the representation might reveal by asking, "How could you represent your thinking so that you can see patterns?"

What Communication Nudges Sound Like

Communication nudges focus on two different forms, oral and written explanation. Students of all ages work on explaining their thinking orally so that others can understand what they have done and why it makes sense. As students get older, they begin to work on how to put these explanations in writing, combining sentences with mathematical representations to provide a clear road map and justification of their thinking. Both forms of explanation are often nudged using similar questions, such as, "How could you explain what you did so that others can understand?" These nudges typically name the audience and form of the explanation, just as representation nudges can. Let's look at an example of using a communication nudge to give students a space to rehearse an explanation before sharing it with the class.

Anne's fourth graders were working on using area models for multiplication of multidigit numbers. She had asked them to find how many 1-square-foot tiles it would take to cover the floor of a room that was 13 feet by 17 feet. Students were using grid paper to draw the room and decompose this multiplication task into rows or columns. Many were struggling to skip count by thirteens or seventeens. When Anne conferred with Samuel and Darius, they had drawn a rectangle and decomposed it into 4 smaller rectangles, found the area of each one, and then added the parts back together. Their strategy made sense mathematically and Anne wanted other students to be able to learn from them, but they had trouble explaining the process and their reasoning clearly. Here is how Anne nudged:

ANNE: You've done some really interesting thinking here and I think you've got an idea that the rest of the class needs to hear. How could you explain this to the class so that other kids can understand what you did?

> *Positioning Students with Competence, The Could Move, and Orienting Students to an Audience*

DARIUS: So we sort of broke it up into some smaller pieces. To make it easier.

SAMUEL: Yeah, but they weren't so small. Before when we were skip counting, thirteens are hard.

DARIUS: So we took out the 10×10, 'cause we know that's 100.

ANNE: Everybody's going to wonder where that 10×10 square came from. How will you show them?

> *Specifying*

DARIUS: Yeah, so we drew a line here and another line here to cut the 2 sides, so that one side is 10 and 3 feet and the other is 10 and 7 feet.

ANNE: So, you decomposed the 2 sides into 10 and 3 instead of 13 feet and 10 and 7 instead of 17 feet.

SAMUEL: Yeah, yeah, that's how we made the 4 rectangles inside it!

ANNE: That's really important. You made 4 rectangles inside the large room. And what did you do with the 4 rectangles?

> *Specifying*

DARIUS: We found the area—.

SAMUEL: Yeah, we found the area. We multiplied them.

ANNE: So, is that what these labels are here, on your paper?

> *Eliciting*

SAMUEL: Yeah, those are the areas.

DARIUS: And we added them up and got 221.

ANNE: 221 what?

> *Specifying*

DARIUS: 221 tiles.

ANNE: Can you share this with the class during the discussion?

This second time through, eliciting Samuel and Darius' thinking, Anne already knows what their process was, and she provides support to help them sequence and explain what they did. She references the class as the audience for their explanation multiple times, and this audience provides a legitimate motivation for constructing a clear and accurate explanation. You'll notice that the students' explanation is still forming; it is not yet a formal, complete explanation. There are plenty of places for the students to add additional detail and reasoning. But this explanation represents a solid second draft, and when they share with the class, they will have an opportunity for a third draft and authentic questions from their peers to help them refine again. Notice also how representation and communication can be intertwined, when the students' representation requires clear explanation to be convincing. This nudge was a rehearsal for sharing, but it could have been a rehearsal for writing instead. Anne could have asked her students to construct written explanations, and nudged Darius and Samuel to say aloud what they planned to write, supporting them to add detail orally before prompting them to write it down.

Communication nudges are opportunities for students to refine and revise their explanations in anticipation of sharing with others, either aloud or in writing. Notice that providing audiences for these explanations creates a real need to describe thinking clearly. The teacher's role is to recognize places where they can support students in being precise or clear, using mathematical language, describing reasoning, or sequencing their process.

What Collaboration Nudges Sound Like

Collaboration nudges deliberately structure the talk between partners equitably, so that all students have a voice and their ideas are considered by the group. The goal is to bring all students together around a plan for moving forward mathematically by supporting them in listening to one another, negotiating, and carving out meaningful ways for each person to participate. Because this nudge is in response to an observed imbalance of participation or lack of joint work, teachers take an active role when nudging collaboration and attempting to get the group back to productive work. These nudges often include prompts for students to revoice what they have heard others say, provide agreement or disagreement and negotiate turns or control over tools. Teachers often make specific statements about the need to come to a shared strategy or decision, the importance of everyone getting to participate and be heard, and the expectation that all students should be able to explain the work of the group.

When we observe a group from afar and see one student at the margins of the work, we often assume that this child is off task, shirking, disengaged, or not participating. This is an assumption that needs to be challenged. It could very well be that the student at the margins is being marginalized. When students' ideas are not considered or taken seriously, their questions not answered, their attempts to participate rebuffed, they withdraw. As you observe groups not yet working collaboratively, it is crucial to examine the entire dynamic of the group to accurately assess the challenge. Let's look at two examples of collaborative nudges, first one in which students are simply working in parallel, and then one in which one partner is being excluded.

Rosario's second graders were working on comparing the lengths of two different objects to find out which was longer and how much longer it was. Students were using a collection of everyday objects from the classroom, such as markers, whiteboard erasers, and pencils. When she approached Julius and Nathan, each partner had two objects and was holding them up next to one another. They were not talking or looking at one another. Each appeared to be working alone, despite being partners. When Rosario elicited their thinking, she confirmed that this was the case. They had each chosen their own objects and were silently comparing them. Here is how Rosario nudged:

ROSARIO: It's important that you both work together to choose two objects and come up with a way to figure out how much longer one is. I see that you each picked your own objects. Now I want you to choose two together. Which two do you want to choose?

> *Orienting to Partners, Prompting Immediate Action, and Noticing Aloud and Asking*

JULIUS: I want to do the magic marker and the dry erase marker.

NATHAN: But I want to do the eraser.

ROSARIO: How are you going to choose?

> *Orienting to Partners*

JULIUS: How 'bout we do this marker and the eraser?

ROSARIO: Nathan, do you agree?

> *Orienting to Partners*

NATHAN: Yeah.

ROSARIO: OK, so you're going to compare these two. How are you going to do it?

> *Orienting to Partners*

NATHAN: I think we should stack up the cubes.

ROSARIO: Julius, do you know what he means when he says, "Stack up the cubes"?

> *Orienting to Partners*

Orienting to Partners —

JULIUS: No.

ROSARIO: So, what are you going to ask him?

JULIUS: What do you mean, "Stack up the cubes"?

NATHAN: Stack up these cubes next to the marker to see how tall. And the same for the eraser.

Orienting to Partners —

ROSARIO: Julius, what did you hear Nathan say?

JULIUS: He said that we should count how many cubes in the stack next to the marker. And then the eraser, too.

NATHAN: Yeah, count the cubes.

Orienting to Partners —

ROSARIO: Nathan, now you want to ask Julius if he agrees with your idea.

NATHAN: Do you agree?

JULIUS: Yeah.

Closing: Encouraging Students to Try Their Ideas —

ROSARIO: Give it a try, together.

Some of this nudge sounds like developing a strategy, but it's important to remember that these two already had strategies when Rosario approached them to confer. They had separate strategies. In this nudge, Rosario makes several moves to get the students talking and listening to one another, orienting to joint work rather than independent work. She offers the students prompts for the kinds of words they might say to one another to explain and negotiate ideas. And she communicates that this is a central part of what they are being asked to do in mathematics. This kind of nudge supports students in coming together by giving them a toehold in collaboration.

Across the room, Rosario encountered a different situation. When she approached Elena and Omar, Elena was hunched over a paper, writing, with all of the objects within the circle of her arms. Omar was sitting back with his arms crossed and his head lowered. When Rosario asked questions about their thinking, only Elena responded. She had lots to say about what she had done. She spoke only to Rosario and did not reference Omar or include him in the conversation. When Rosario asked Omar about what he was thinking, he said, "She won't let me." Here is how Rosario nudged:

Noticing Aloud and Asking and Orienting to Partners —

ROSARIO: Elena, I notice that your partner doesn't have a way to participate in the work. You have all the tools. What can we do about that?

(Elena pushes some of the objects toward Omar.)

ELENA: Here.

ROSARIO: OK, that's a start. When we're doing math, everybody needs to get to participate. One way we can do that is by sharing the materials. Why don't we put everything in the middle?

(Elena puts the paper and pencil in the middle.)

ROSARIO: Omar, do you remember what the task is for today?   Retelling and Orienting to Partners

OMAR: Yeah, to choose two things and see how much longer one is.

ROSARIO: Elena, do you agree that that's what we're doing today?   Orienting to Partners

ELENA: Yeah.

ROSARIO: Great. So, what's the first thing you two need to do together?   Retelling, Orienting to Partners, and Prompting Immediate Action

OMAR: Choose two things.

ELENA: Yeah.

(Long pause as Omar and Elena look at Rosario. Rosario waits.)

ELENA: The pencil?

OMAR: Yeah, and the marker.

ELENA: OK.

ROSARIO: I really appreciate how you two came to agreement about the objects. Now, what?   Orienting to Partners and Prompting Immediate Action

OMAR: Measure how tall.

ELENA: Yeah, we can lay down the cubes.

OMAR: Yeah, OK.

ROSARIO: OK, it sounds like you have a plan. I'll be back to check in with you guys in a bit.   Closing: Encouraging Students to Try Their Ideas

Rosario uses some similar moves in this nudge, such as checking for agreement and directing her talk to individual students. However, she makes deliberate moves to structure their interaction for equity, by naming the importance of everyone getting to participate and pointing to some concrete ways of making that possible. Rosario uses wait time here to prompt the students to figure out what two objects they would choose together, resisting the temptation to tell them how or do it for them. This kind of collaboration nudge takes a dysfunctional dynamic that interfered with mathematics and got it back on track. It is worth noting, though, that these students might very well encounter collaborative challenges again. Status is a stubborn thing to level. In this moment, Omar and Elena are working together, but they may slip back into an inequitable pattern of interaction again—particularly when they legitimately disagree about the mathematics —and need another nudge.

Collaboration nudges, like the two examples shown here, can require many teacher moves to restructure the collaborative dynamic. Students may need model language for how to talk to one another, prompts to revoice and listen closely to other's ideas, and explicit messages that you value collaboration. These nudges offer the opportunity to bring students together, in the moment, for joint work, forming a bridge between what you have discussed with the whole class and the specific challenges that emerge when children try it. Making collaborative problem-solving work means supporting students through these sticky moments.

These examples of how nudges can sound are meant to illustrate some possibilities, rather than be prescriptive. The moves described in this chapter can be used in unlimited combinations to gently advance student thinking down these five pathways for nudging. Choosing your moves is hard work, though, precisely because nudging happens so quickly. In the next chapter, we'll turn to some common challenges teachers face when conferring, and ideas for how to address them in the moment.

COMMON QUESTIONS

What do I do if I get stuck?

It may happen that you start to nudge, and it does not feel like it is working, or you may sense that you've lost your way. Occasionally, you might sense that you've wandered into a conversational cul-de-sac, and you're circling endlessly with nowhere to go. If you get stuck, lost, or confused, the most useful thing to do is often to circle back to eliciting again. Go back to what students were doing when you arrived. Ask them questions to clarify whatever miscommunications may have arisen. Give yourself a chance to think through the signals in what students share. Use Figure 4.1 to help you choose a nudge, and try again. We'll talk about this in more detail in the next chapter.

The students in this group need very different things. What do I nudge?

There are a couple of different ways to think about this dilemma. If you sense that the students in the group are in different places, it may well be that students need a collaboration nudge. Students will still bring different kinds of understanding to collaboration. This is an asset of working together; students have different wells of knowledge and ideas to draw on. However, if one student is stuck figuring out the task, while the other is considering ways to represent thinking, then fundamentally it is collaboration that has broken down. Another way to think about this dilemma is to consider which kind of nudge will allow the entire group to move forward. For instance, if one member is confused about the task and another is ready to think about strategies, nudging conceptual understanding by helping all students to get access to the meaning of the task will allow the group to think about strategy next. In this case, conceptual understanding is the gatekeeper. If you were to nudge developing a strategy, you would exclude the confused student from the group's future work.

What do I do when students develop a plan that won't work or is flawed?

Mistakes are how we learn. If you nudge students and they develop a strategy or plan for their next steps that you can clearly see is flawed, it often makes sense to let them try it and learn from what happens. Encourage students to try their plan, and commit to coming back to see how it went, anticipating that at that point they will have encountered the very challenge you foresee, and they will then need you to nudge them to think about what it means and what to try next.

REFLECTING ON YOUR OWN PRACTICE

As you think about getting started with conferring, the following guiding questions might help you reflect on how you try to advance students' thinking:

- How do these nudges sound like how you currently try to advance your students' thinking? What's different or new?

- What do you tend to focus your attention on when you try to advance students' thinking?
- What opportunities in your classroom are there to nudge conceptual thinking, developing a strategy, representation, communication, or collaboration?
- What types of nudges would you like to try? Can you think of moments in your classroom where they might have been useful?
- As you get started nudging, what will you have to pay attention to decide what kind of nudge students need?
- Which of the nudging moves do you already use? What variations would you like to try out? Which other moves would you like to add to your tool kit? You may want to jot down some ideas to carry around with you to draw on in the moment.

5

Common Challenges

Conferring is challenging because you never know precisely how it will go until you are in the moment with students. Students do and say unexpected things. You might notice a misunderstanding and begin to feel like you're pulling teeth to get students back on track. You might have carefully chosen a nudge only to be met with blank stares. You might form an interpretation of student thinking only to have students tell you no, that's not what we meant. In these moments, you might feel lost or even like you're playing tug-of-war with students, rather than collaborating with them. What's going on? And what do you do about it?

In this chapter, we'll dig into three common challenges, and how to recognize them. I will then offer three strategies for getting a conference back on track. Each of these strategies involves lines of questioning that can help teachers and students come to shared understanding of the task, what students currently think, and where they want to go.

Three Signs a Conference Needs a New Direction

First, we will examine a common and unproductive questioning pattern called "funneling," which can fool us into believing the conversation has supported learning when it has not. Second, what if your attempts to nudge are met with confusion? We will look at clues that a nudge has missed its mark and is not being taken up by students. Third, students sometimes push back, and this is important to notice because it can allow us to get the conference onto a more productive pathway.

Pulling Teeth: Funneling

When conferring gets frustrating, I often hear teachers describe it as pulling teeth. By this they mean that they are trying to get students to do or say something, to get somewhere, and the kids are simply not cooperating, not seeing what the teachers see, and not making the connections teachers want them to make. Behind this feeling is great intent: we want students to learn and we're looking for evidence in what they say that they understand. And, of course, students don't always understand. Pulling teeth is what happens when students are struggling, and teachers try to support them by using an unproductive questioning pattern called funneling (Wood 1998).

Funneling involves asking a series of closed questions that are designed to get students to say something specific, but these questions ignore that students do not understand the meaning of their responses. The questions get narrower and narrower to get students to say what teachers want to hear, until students do. It's a lot of work to ask these questions to funnel students into the right words, which is why it feels like pulling teeth. Let's look at an example of funneling in action and then unpack why it is unproductive for learning.

In Callie's fourth-grade classroom, the students were solving a problem that involved sharing 45 crackers equally among 6 friends. When she approached a pair of students they were struggling to decide how to get started with the task, and they were discussing multiplying the two numbers, 45 and 6, to find the answer, but they were concerned by how much work this was going to be. Here's what Callie did to funnel them away from multiplication and toward division as the appropriate operation:

CALLIE: What operation should we use when we want to make equal shares?

ENRIQUE: Multiplication?

CALLIE: Multiplication? We use multiplication?

ENRIQUE: Addition?

CALLIE: But we know we want to make the group smaller, right? To share with the friends? So what operation do we use to make a group smaller?

SARAH: Subtraction?

CALLIE: Would subtraction work?

ENRIQUE: Yeah?

CALLIE: But here we're *dividing* the group of crackers into small groups. Not just taking away. So, what do we do when we're dividing the group up?

SARAH: Division?

CALLIE: Division. Yes, we divide. Right?

Callie gets Sarah to say, "Division," but a close look at the interaction makes it clear that neither Enrique nor Sarah know what operation to use or why. The interaction functions like a multiple-choice test with the teacher eliminating possibilities until there is only one correct answer left. Funneling like this sometimes ends with teachers asking very closed questions to get students to say just the thing they want to hear, as Callie does here. The final question in funneling might be pointing to a problem and saying, "What number is this?" or leading students to guess with, "It starts with an *M*. . . ." The focus of these questions is simply to get students to say the words we want to hear, and we can be very good at constructing these funneling sequences to achieve this goal. But it's the wrong goal.

Funneling is unproductive for student learning for two key reasons. First, as with Sarah and Enrique in the vignette, getting students to say something does not mean they understand it. Students are not reasoning about mathematics anymore; they are engaged in a guessing game about what their teacher is thinking. Students likely do not understand how to apply what they have said to the task at hand. For instance, Enrique and Sarah may not know which numbers to divide or how to do that division, and they very likely would not know how to transfer the underlying idea of making equal groups through division to other similar problems. Conferring is meant to support students in building understanding through careful reasoning about mathematics, and funneling divorces the conversation from reasoning, undermining this intent.

Second, funneling fools us as teachers into thinking students understand when they do not. It serves as false formative assessment data. If Callie were to walk away from conferring with Sarah and Enrique believing that they now understood how to solve equal shares problems by dividing, she might not provide the instructional supports that they still need to make sense out of these tasks. She might falsely think that they were struggling productively when they are, in fact, still stuck. I have often heard teachers say with dismay that they thought their students understood a concept until they gave a formal assessment, only to discover many misconceptions. Funneling may play a role in this flawed sense of students' understandings during conferring. It is important to acknowledge that funneling, although unproductive, is incredibly common, and every teacher (and parent) has engaged in this pattern of interaction before. But when we are focused on supporting student reasoning, we must learn to recognize when we lapse into funneling and stop it in its tracks.

Signs You May Be Funneling

You may be funneling if you are trying to get students to say something specific and you feel yourself asking narrow questions to get those words to come out of their mouths. Your own frustration or the sense of pulling teeth is another strong clue. Finally, after students say just the right thing, you may hear them push back. For instance, after Callie funneled Enrique and Sarah, Sarah responded with, "But divide *what*?" to express her continued confusion. We'll look more closely at pushing back in a later section.

The Blank Stare: When a Nudge Goes Nowhere

RESPONDING TO THE BLANK STARE

5.1 Mary reflects on moments when she has received the blank stare, how she interprets this signal, and what she does next to get the conversation going again.

Sometimes you might ask a question or start to nudge and be met with a blank stare. It's important to keep in mind that students need wait time, so silence itself is not a warning sign. But if you wait and nothing happens, or students make doubtful or noncommittal responses, such as, "Uhh . . ." or "Yeah . . . ," then this indicates that students are not taking up your question. They may not understand what you mean, or you may be pointing them down a pathway that is very different from the one they had in mind. Something in the conversation has become unhitched so that students are no longer following you. Let's look at a pair of examples from Grace's first-grade classroom.

Grace's students were working on decomposing 20 using a rekenrek, a bead frame with 2 rows of 10 beads. One partner would hide some of the beads behind a piece of paper and then ask the other how many were missing, and how they knew. When Grace approached Sione and Jessica, Grace learned that Jessica had hidden 12 beads and Sione knew this because 1 whole row was missing and 2 more. Then Grace posed a completely new question, "Can you write a number sentence to show what you just did?" This could have been a representation nudge, but the students didn't take it up. Instead, they just stared at Grace. This could mean that the students weren't yet ready to think about representing their thinking using symbols or that they were confused by the idea of taking their hiding game and making it a number sentence. When Grace asked a similar question of two students on the other side of the room a little later in the work time, Marcus replied, "I guess so" and then stopped. Grace waited but the students offered no ideas for what this number sentence might be. She then asked, "What could the number sentence look like?" to which Marcus replied, "I don't know." In both of these instances, the students do not meaningfully take up Grace's suggestion that they represent their work with symbols.

These are critical moments to explore. Although it appears that students are confused, it is actually the teacher who has misunderstood something about the students' thinking. Rather than plunging ahead with the teacher's idea, which ultimately means taking over the students' work, confronting little or no uptake means that the conversation needs to rewind a bit to correct the teacher's interpretation. In the examples from Grace's classroom, if she chose to move forward with writing a number sentence, she might end up funneling students by asking narrow questions about each element of the number sentence. However, it may be more productive to back up and ask more broadly about ways they could represent what they did on paper, recognizing that the leap to symbols was too great at this moment.

Signs of Little or No Student Uptake

Lack of student uptake can be seen in a blank, deer-in-the-headlights look, or heard in silence or hesitant, nonsubstantive responses, like "Uh-huh" or "I guess." The tone is crucial in reading students' uptake. Listen for doubt, or the possibility that students might be saying what they think you want to hear. Be sure to offer plenty of wait time; students may just need to think about your question or idea. But if wait time settles into silence, it is time to ask yourself what you may have misinterpreted.

Pushback: When We're on the Wrong Path

Part of conferring is making our interpretations of students' thinking public and offering avenues for students to pursue. In doing so, we may misstep, and students will let us know by pushing back. Pushing back means that students want to understand and be understood. Student pushback is a positive signal that students have agency over their own learning, and they are using their own authority to express that something is not working for them in an interaction (Munson 2016).

As teachers it is important for all of us to figure out what is happening when students push back. Students push back in two circumstances. First, students often push back at the end of funneling. Students will participate in the funnel, answering teachers' ever-narrowing questions that point toward the desired response. But afterward, that may ask a question that shows that they still don't understand what to do or why it makes sense. In this way, pushback and funneling go hand in hand, and we should greet pushback as useful feedback from students that we haven't been supporting their reasoning.

Second, students push back when they feel that they have been ignored or misunderstood. Again, this is a welcome sign that students want to partner with us as we elicit and form an interpretation of their thinking. They want to be understood and heard, and they legitimately feel that conferring is a venue for furthering their learning. When we think about nudges being a joint project, pushback is a critical part of negotiating that nudge and hearing when and whether we are getting to that learning together.

Let's look at examples of each of these in turn.

I Don't Understand

After Callie funneled Enrique and Sarah into saying division, Sarah responded by saying, "But divide *what*?" She was communicating a desire to understand why and how division could be used—and that she didn't yet have this understanding. Simply guessing the operation isn't the same as understanding the concepts behind its application. Confusion—and a desire to understand—underlie the meaning of student pushback in this moment. In another example from the same class, students in a group had become tangled up in their numbers and lost track of how many groups and how many crackers they had when sharing the 45 crackers. As Callie tried to guide them to notice what they had been doing by walking through their calculations, one student voiced, "But it's so confusing. But is 6 the crackers or the groups?" He was signaling that he had lost meaning in the calculations and needed to go back to consider what each number represented. Students use this form of pushback to advocate for their own understanding and ask for help.

You Don't Understand Me

When misunderstanding goes the opposite way, students attempt to signal the miscommunication by pushing back. Students may be saying several subtly different things: "I disagree," "You didn't hear me," or "That's not what I need." Regardless of the specific message, students push back to communicate that they do not feel understood and they are attempting to clarify. In Callie's class, she conferred with a pair of students who were making groups of 6 crackers to solve the problem of sharing 45 crackers equally among 6 friends.

CALLIE: The story tells us that there are 6 friends sharing crackers. How can you show the 6 *groups*?

BRANDON: But we are!

CALLIE: I see you putting 6 *crackers*.

BRANDON: Yeah, but that's 'cause we know 6 times 6. 6 times 6 is 36.

FOA: Yeah, we're doing those first.

BRANDON: Then the leftovers.

Callie made an understandable interpretation that the students were mistaken about what the 6 in the story represented. She tried to get the students to revise their strategy to focus on making 6 groups of crackers, but the students pushed back saying that they did understand this and were instead using a known fact to decompose the problem. Notice how the students use *but* as a way of expressing their pushback. Brandon pushed back twice, first with a protest and then with more detail that makes the misunderstanding clear. Students often use this form of pushback to address what they see as faulty assumptions about their work. They may push back if you assume from your brief glimpse at their work that they have been unproductive or not collaborating; they may push back if your interpretation of their thinking is flawed or incomplete.

Signs Students Are Pushing Back

Pushback always says, "No," in some way. It often starts with, "But . . ." and may sound like a protest. This disagreement can contribute to a sense that you are pulling teeth or battling with students. Conferring should be a partnership. When it instead feels like tug-of-war, it is time for a reassessment of the different goals each person has and what students are trying to tell you. Remember that pushback is positive, a sign that students are invested in their own understanding and that they believe that you want to understand their thinking.

Listening for these signs of funneling, lack of uptake, and pushback gives teachers the opportunity to change the direction of the conversation so that a nudge is possible, and everyone leaves the conference feeling that they have learned something. In the next section, we'll look at how to change direction to get conferring back on track.

How to Get Back on Track

Once you notice that a conference is becoming unproductive, what can you do? Conferring is a conversation, and like any conversation, anyone can shift its trajectory at any point. There are three strategies you can try to get conferring back on track toward productively advancing student thinking: anchor to the task, elicit more, or anchor to student work. Let's take a look at each strategy, when you might choose it, and how to give it a try.

Anchor to the Task

When miscommunication strikes, one place that can serve as common ground is the task. Anchoring to the task means returning to the text or substance of the problem that launched the work for the day. This allows you and students to ensure that you all have a shared understanding of what students have been asked to do. Often this can help you trace how students are making sense of the task and identify any places where your understandings diverge. When students are reporting how they are reasoning about a problem, they may be so far down a solution pathway that it is hard to understand how they got to where they are. Returning to the task allows everyone to agree on a starting point and tell the story of reasoning sequentially.

When to Choose This Strategy

Anchor to the task when it is clear that you and students are not understanding one another. You may have asked a question and received the blank stare or confronted pushback that makes you think that you and your students do not have a shared understanding of what is going on in the task or in their work. Starting from the beginning allows you to begin with something in common and build from there.

Moves to Try

Moves that support students on understanding the meaning of the task and connecting it to their own thinking will anchor everyone to the task. This includes retelling moves, like those discussed in Chapter 4, and moves that prompt students to visualize the story, act it out, or make connections between the task and the work they have done. These moves can sound like:

- **RETELLING:** What is happening in the story? Can you tell me what the task is?
- **VISUALIZING:** Describe what's happening. What does it look like? Where are the _____ ? Paint a picture of what is going on.
- **ACT IT OUT:** Let's act it out. Who's going to be _____ ? I'll be _____ . Tell me what to do.
- **CONNECTING THE TASK TO STUDENT WORK:** Where is this part of the story in your work? How does this (manipulative, drawing, number sentence, etc.) show the story (or match the task)?

As students retell, visualize, act out, or connect their work to the story, you may discover how students are making sense of the task and in doing so form a more accurate interpretation of their thinking than you had before. This will allow you to choose a nudge that better matches what students are ready for next.

Elicit More

Eliciting more is a near-foolproof way of straightening out a challenging interaction. It means exactly what it sounds like; you circle back to the beginning of conferring by asking more questions that surface students' thinking, which can provide you with additional information with which to build a robust interpretation of student thinking. Your eliciting questions may be more focused on probing for reasoning or on specific areas of student thinking that are the source of miscommunication. For instance, in the conference in which Brandon pushed back on Callie about the strategy he and his partner were using to represent equal groups, Callie might then want to ask questions about how they decided on their approach and what they plan to do next. These would likely be different questions than she asked before because she is following up on new information.

When to Choose This Strategy

Eliciting more can be used in nearly any situation, but it is particularly useful following student pushback or when recovering from funneling. In one study I conducted, the only instance of a conference still leading to a nudge after funneling was when a teacher followed up with the question, "Does that make sense?" When she saw the confusion on her students' faces, she began asking eliciting questions that got the conference centered back on student reasoning rather than guessing.

Moves to Try

To elicit more you can use any of the moves described in Chapter 3. It can be useful to lean into probing for reasoning questions to make sure that you understand not just what students did but why and how it made sense to them. You can ask students to circle back to the beginning of what they did and describe their thinking in a complete sequential explanation. This can help if you feel that you got the story of students' thinking out of order and in ways that may have contributed to you filling in the gaps inaccurately. Or, you can focus your eliciting questions on the specific parts of students' work that seem to be gumming up your understanding or the interaction. These moves are particularly helpful when following up on pushback. For instance, if students say, "But that's not what we did," you can elicit more by asking, "So what did you do?"

Anchor to Student Work

One of the challenging parts of conferring is the number of different storylines that you must coordinate as you try to interpret student thinking. You must reconcile your own understanding of the task, what each student says to you, and, in many cases, their written or physical representation of their work. At times these don't seem to agree, and conflicts between different forms of information can lead you to make assumptions about what students really meant or what they really did. These assumptions can ultimately prove to be flawed in ways that cause confusion, pushback, or blank stares. Anchoring to student work means that you physically point out aspects of students' work—on paper, with manipulatives, or gestures like counting on fingers—that you want students to explain to you in greater detail. By targeting your questions to specific areas of their work that don't yet make sense to you or are the subject of pushback, you can uncover student thinking that you missed or misunderstood.

When to Choose This Strategy

Anchor to student work when you can identify specific parts of their representations that conflict or confuse. You may realize your misunderstanding following a blank stare or student pushback, or you may have been confused all along by the mismatch between your interpretations of what students said and their physical representations of the mathematics.

Moves to Try

Anchoring to student work is a very targeted form of eliciting. Identify a specific aspect of students' work that you believe to be contributing to the confusion or disagreement in your conference. This can be anything visible, such as a drawing, numbers, symbols, manipulatives, a point on a graph, the students' use of fingers, or even a gesture. Point this feature out, drawing everyone's attention to it, and then ask a specific question about what it means, where it comes from, or its connection to what students have said, the story, or other parts of the work. These pointed questions might sound like:

- What does this (number, symbol, drawing) mean? What does it represent?
- Where did it come from? How did you decide to use it?
- How does this (drawing, manipulative, representation) help you? How are you using it?
- How is this (number, symbol, drawing, manipulative) connected to the story?
- How is this (number, symbol, drawing, manipulative) related to what you just told me you did?
- How is this part of your work connected to this other part?

These questions make students' thinking clearer and may also help students make connections between their words, numbers, drawing, and the task (as with moves connecting the task to student work described earlier). As you ask these targeted questions, you may uncover the source of students' pushback or your own confusion that lead you to more fruitful questions and a more accurate interpretation of what students did and why.

Keep Your Purpose in Mind

No matter how much experience teachers have with conferring, there will always come an interaction that makes it challenging to respond or where confusion sets in. Getting back on track is far easier to do, however, when you keep the purpose of conferring in mind. Conferring should support you to learn about students' thinking and students in growing their thinking from wherever they are. Conferring places students' ideas at the center of discussion. Missteps are more likely when teachers focus on getting kids to finish a task, come to a particular idea or answer, or arrive at a predetermined outcome. If you find yourself feeling rigid about what you want kids to do, say, or think, refocus your thinking on what kids *are* doing, saying, or thinking and take it from there. If you feel confused, feel free to tell kids just that. If you have designed tasks to support inquiry, then your students spend a lot of time in productive struggle, and it is powerful for you to model that you experience this struggle, too. Pinpoint your confusion, ask a question, and listen hard to the response. Stay curious.

COMMON QUESTIONS

What if I get conflicting signals from different students in the same group?

You may find that one student pushes back while another does not, or that two students stare blankly while a third is ready to answer. When conferring, one key goal is building shared understanding, between you and the students and among partners. If any student sends signals that something in the conference is not working for them, it is worth attending to. You can name this explicitly, by saying something like, "I hear that you are ready to talk about this idea, but it sounds like your partner disagrees. Tell us about your thinking. What did I miss?" or "I notice that your partners look confused. I want to make sure we all understand what we're talking about. What are you guys thinking?" Notice that these are both strategies that focus on more eliciting, but that they do it by framing how important every student's contribution is to shared work. Even if one partner is voluble and makes themselves the center of conversation, you must not ignore the quiet protest or resistance of a partner. To do so would be to marginalize the worthiness of their thinking and, ultimately, their learning.

What do I do if we're all confused and frustrated?

Take a deep breath. Focus on what you think you understand. If that feels like very little, go back to the beginning and anchor to the task. What is the problem about? What are students trying? Every student understands something, and they are using that understanding to make decisions. Your goal is to find the sense in what they are doing. It is there. Partner with students. Name how hard this is. You might say, "Wow. This is hard work. I can feel myself getting frustrated because I really want to understand what you're thinking, and I don't understand yet. Are you feeling frustrated, too? Can we start again from the beginning?" If you think you have meddled in students' work by funneling or trying to control what they do and that is why everyone is frustrated, you can say that and try to rewind a bit back to the last moment when students seemed to feel confident. You could say, "I think I've messed you up with all my questions. Can we rewind? You told me _____. Can you tell me more about that?" Students are often forgiving and flexible, particularly when they hear how important their thinking is to you and that conferring is not a test they are failing. Affirm that this conversation is a partnership and you are in it with them, confident that together you all can understand one another and that their learning is worth all this work.

REFLECTING ON YOUR OWN PRACTICE

As you think about challenges you might confront when conferring, the following guiding questions might help you reflect on your practice:

- What does it feel like to you when conferring is not going well? What signals are students sending you? What might they mean?
- When do you funnel? What does it sound or feel like when you are funneling?
- What does student pushback sound like in your classroom? When do you hear it?
- How will you listen for signs that conferring has gotten off track?
- What signs that conferring is off track do you hear most often? What goals might this help you set?
- What strategies do you want to try when you sense that conferring is off track? What will you need to help you practice?
- How can you tell when you've gotten a conference back on track? What did you do to right the ship?

6

Using Conferring as Formative Assessment

ormative assessment is the process of finding out where students are in their learning while they are learning, rather than at some endpoint, like the end of the unit or year. Formative assessment has been shown to have a powerful impact on student learning (Black and Wiliam 1998) and should be a daily part of every classroom. Often when we think of formative assessment, we think of exit tickets or the daily work completed in class, or even homework and quizzes. But the conferences we have with students are formative assessment, too. Indeed, conferring is formative assessment at its most immediate, relevant, and useful, because we can act on what we learn immediately in the nudge. With a bit more planning we can act on what we learn while conferring in many more ways that make all of our instruction more responsive and powerful.

Using conferring data as formative assessment involves four key stages: gathering conferring data, reflecting on that data, planning for how to respond, and responding through instruction.

So far in this book we have focused on the first stage, in which teachers learn about their students' thinking in the moment through eliciting and nudging. Now we turn to the next three stages.

In this chapter, we'll explore four ways to use conferring data to inform instruction, and for each we'll consider guiding questions to support reflecting on the data gathered in conferences and planning instructional responses. Throughout the chapter you'll find examples of how Faith and Mary reflect on the conferring data they have gathered in their second- and fourth-grade classrooms and think through how they might respond to emerging observations and trends. Finally, to support using conferring data as formative assessment, we will take a brief look at record keeping, with templates provided in the appendix.

Four Ways to Use Conferring to Inform Instruction

What we learn in conferences can be used to accomplish the following:

1. Focus the closing discussion for the day.
2. Inform conferences with the same students on future days.
3. Shape the next day's lesson or tasks.
4. Anticipate students' struggles and strategies for the next day.

Focusing the Closing Discussion

After students have had a chance to engage in the mathematical task you have selected for the day and you have conferred with a number of students, you will likely bring the class together for a closing discussion or debrief of what students learned. These discussions should have a preplanned focus that aligns with your instructional goal for the day. However, precisely how you discuss the mathematical ideas you had in mind will depend on the actual work students have done during the work time. Students may have invented new strategies, found a pattern, developed new representations, or struggled to make sense of ideas. At the end of the work time and before the discussion, step back and consider what trends exist in your conferring for the day, what intriguing ideas or questions emerged, and how you'd like to respond to students' thinking in the whole-group context of the discussion.

Guiding Questions for Planning the Closing Discussion

To use conferring to shape the closing discussion, consider the following reflection questions:

- What trends existed in students' thinking or strategies? What does the class as a whole seem to understand? Not yet understand?
- What surprising things did students do, try, think, or ask?
- How did the strategies or ideas that you saw during conferring connect to your instructional goals for the day?
- Were there any new ways of representing thinking that emerged?
- What aspects of the student work that you saw or discussed would be useful for the whole class to see?
- Did any misconceptions emerge? Is it likely that other groups encountered those same misconceptions? Is it important to address those misconceptions immediately?
- How diverse were the strategies students used? What could the class gain from seeing that variety?
- Did students pose any questions or encounter any struggles that it would be useful for the class to grapple with?

In the brief moments after finishing your last conference and calling the class together, you may not have time to reflect on all of these questions. But with practice, you can learn to notice features that surface during conferring that you want to incorporate in the discussion, whether they are ideas from individual interactions or trends across the class. (Both are important!)

Ways to Respond to Student Thinking Through the Discussion

After reflecting on your conferring, you may want to tailor the closing discussion in one of several ways, depending on whether you want to focus the class' attention on something from a specific conference, or ideas you saw surfacing repeatedly while conferring. You might:

- Highlight a specific idea that emerged from one of your conferences. You might tell the story of your interaction and let the students share their thinking with the class. This is particularly useful if you want the class to learn from what one group tried, such as creating a new strategy or representation, or untangling a misconception.

- Raise a sticky question that emerged from one or more of your conferences. At times conferring reveals a conceptual hurdle that is difficult to resolve in a single brief conference. Such challenges often get at big underlying mathematical ideas. Students in a partnership may disagree and be unable to fully resolve the mathematical argument. It could be that the same confusion is proving challenging for multiple groups. Bringing the debate or confusion to the whole class provides more time for discussion, recruits more participants with other ways to think about the conflict, and creates an opportunity for everyone to learn from the disagreement.

- Invite students to share diverse strategies or answers from the day's task. Often there is much for the class to learn from seeing multiple strategies or answers, making connections between them, and looking for patterns. You may want to invite students to share different ways of solving problems for the express purpose of discussing what they have in common, how they are different, which are more or less efficient, or how they could be used in combination. For tasks with multiple answers, the discussion may take the form of pooling and justifying answers from across the class to make patterns more visible.

- Prompt the class to reflect on their processes or state of learning. The discussion can be a powerful place to promote metacognition (awareness of one's own thinking, learning, and processes). If the class encountered a specific and unexpected frustration or challenge during the lesson which you noticed repeatedly while conferring, you might ask students questions in the

REFLECTIONS ON FOCUSING THE CLOSING DISCUSSION

 Mary uses conferring data to inform how she orchestrates her closing discussions, which she calls the *debrief*. In this video clip, listen to how Mary reflects on her own process for making decisions about structuring the discussion based on what she learns about student thinking and strategies during the work time.

discussion that get them to reflect on what contributed to the challenge, how it felt, and what the class might do about it the next day. Conversely, if something about the ways students were working was significantly smoother or more comfortable compared with previous days, you may want to ask students to articulate how they accomplished this or what supported them.

Planning whole-class mathematics discussions is an entire area of pedagogy worth exploring in its own right. To learn more, I encourage you to explore Smith and Stein's excellent book, *5 Practices for Orchestrating Productive Mathematics Discussions* (2011).

Informing Future Conferences with the Same Students

Another way to think about conferring is that it is not just the story of a single lesson but the story of individual students over time. Conferring provides a glimpse at how students are thinking at a given moment. If teachers can consider how a student was thinking yesterday, last week, the week before, and so on, they can create a picture of a single student's learning trajectory. Understanding the arc of an individual student's learning can help teachers identify growth, recognize opportunities to push that student forward, and notice ways that the student may be getting stuck. Over time conferring accumulates into a nuanced picture of each student's learning, providing detailed, real-time formative assessment data. However, to make use of this long view, teachers need to rely on more than memory. Teachers need records they can refer back to as they consider how what they saw today fits into the larger story of a child's learning. Later in the chapter we'll look at some ideas for how you might keep records of your conferences so that you can see precisely where students have come from and document change over a unit or year.

Guiding Questions for Reflecting on a Student's Learning Trajectory

As you confer with students, consider the following questions to identify ways to connect this one conference to a student's (or group's) longer learning trajectory:

- How is the student's thinking similar to the last time you conferred with them? What has changed? How?

- If the student is thinking in very similar ways to your last interaction, how long have they been in this same conceptual place? Could they be stuck and need a nudge to try something new or more efficient?
- If the student is trying something new, what does this tell you about their growth? Does it make sense to notice this growth aloud so students pay attention to its value?
- How is the student's patterns of participation similar to or different from the last few times you conferred with them? For instance, are they always leading the work, or always on the margins? How might you disrupt patterns that seem inequitable?
- What understanding does this particular student need to move forward—not just in this problem but in the arc of their learning?

Conferring interactions are so brief that it can be easy to assume that we don't learn much about any individual student. These interactions are just snapshots. However, when taken together, over the course of weeks and months, these snapshots can become a flip-book if we learn how to assemble them together.

Ways to Connect Conferring from One Day to Another

As you confer you may notice things about students' thinking or engagement that make you wonder if they are important or fleeting. For instance, if a student is quiet, this could be just a momentary occurrence, a sign of inequitable group dynamics, or an indication of confusion. You may decide to act right then to elicit, probe, and nudge, or what you notice may simply be something you want to keep an eye on over time. Keeping records over time allows you to develop and test ideas about students that can help you make decisions about what they need. (See page 109 for more on this.)

When you do choose to act, it is useful to make an explicit connection between what you are noticing in the current conference and what you've seen in the past, before using that connection to nudge. That might sound like, "I'm noticing that you're using the same strategy that you've been using for the last few weeks. It seems to work for you, but I'm also noticing that it takes a while. I'm wondering if there is a way to make your strategy more efficient." Or "I've noticed that when you all work together, Marco always does the recording and he's the one who answers my questions. It's important that everyone gets the chance to speak and try to write your ideas. How could you do that?"

Shaping the Next Day's Lesson

After you confer with students during work time, trends in their thinking can help you in deciding what experiences the class needs next to move their thinking forward. It is difficult to know in advance precisely how long it will take students to understand a new concept or to develop increasingly accurate and efficient strategies. You may know that you have approximately three weeks for a unit on geometry, and you likely have clear goals for that unit. But as you move from day to day, pacing how long you stay with each idea and how to move students forward are decisions best informed by your assessment of what the class understands today. Reflecting on the data you gathered about the class as a whole during conferring can help you make these decisions about the task you select (or have selected) for the next day.

Guiding Questions for Planning the Next Day's Lesson

When reflecting on where students are, you'll want to consider both your conferring and the class's discussion as formative assessment data:

- What do students understand? Not yet understand? What are students poised to try next?
- What misconceptions arose? How are students thinking through those ideas now? Do they need another opportunity to tackle these ideas?
- How challenged were students today? Were students struggling productively, or stuck?
- What aspects of today's task challenged students? What aspects were largely comfortable?
- What are students ready for?

Responding to Students' Thinking Through the Next Task

After reflecting on conferring and the day's closing discussion, you'll want to consider the mathematical work you plan to engage students in the following day. If you already have a task planned, you may want to adapt it.

HOW CONFERRING CAN SHAPE THE NEXT LESSON

6.2 In this clip, Mary has just engaged her fourth graders in a lesson as part of a unit on subtraction. In the lesson, the students keep track of the inventory of a T-shirt factory as shirts are made and sold (Fosnot 2008). Mary had noticed at the beginning of this unit that her students used the traditional algorithm for subtraction but did not understand why it worked or what the numbers represented. Her goal was to support them in connecting the algorithm they already knew with other representations of subtraction to build meaning. The task she gave them on this day was to check whether or not the following solution for the inventory, made by a fictitious student, was correct, if the factory had 1,707 T-shirts and sold 550 of them.

$$\begin{array}{r} 1{,}707 \\ -\ 550 \\ \hline 1{,}257 \end{array}$$

Mary placed base ten blocks on the board to represent the 1,707 T-shirts so students could see the starting amount. They were then asked to work in partnerships to use the base ten blocks as evidence for whether or not the student's work was correct. During conferring, Mary encountered students who were deeply frustrated and confused. In the video, notice how Mary thinks through the data she gathered through conferring, what she learned in the closing discussion, and how she plans to use that data to shape her plans for the next day's lesson. Note also how Mary generates some theories about what may be causing her students' frustration and plans her work for the next day to help her test her ideas and learn more, developing her own pedagogical content knowledge (see page 108) as she does so.

If you are planning from scratch, you'll want to consider how tomorrow's task should connect with today's. You might want to:

- Design a task very similar to today's task if you believe students need more time exploring the ideas introduced or worked on today.

- Alter the numbers in the kind of task to change the level of challenge or the kinds of patterns students can notice.

- Apply the same concept to a new or unfamiliar context to help students transfer their understanding and see how ideas generalize.

- Grapple with a question or misconception that surfaced during today's work by crafting a task that foregrounds this idea. This might include specifically naming the debate or confusion and asking students to do some work to resolve it.

- Encourage students to try out an idea that emerged from conferring and was shared in the discussion. For instance, you might choose a task that invites students to try a new strategy, representation, or manipulative, or you may simply keep the same task you had already planned but introduce it by encouraging students to try out what they saw the previous day.

- Refocus the purpose of tomorrow's task from focusing on solving the problem to developing more efficient strategies, creating representations, or articulating clear arguments. This makes sense if students can get to an answer but their engagement in these practices needs further growth.

You may find that there are even more ways to adapt or craft the next day's work to respond to the ideas that you uncovered while conferring. By asking how tomorrow could build on today, you are actively building mathematical connections and providing the kind of responsive instruction that has been shown to boost student learning.

> **HOW CONFERRING CAN SHAPE THE NEXT LESSON**
>
> **6.3** In this clip, Faith reflects on what she learned about her second-grade students' understanding after a lesson in which they worked on counting classroom objects in groups of tens and loose ones and then recording their findings numerically. For instance, 7 packs of 10 markers and 9 loose ones would be written as *79*. The class had been doing this sort of counting for several days to support making connections between counting, place value, and written numbers. Faith describes some examples of what she observed while conferring and what she plans to try the next day to respond to ideas that emerged in two of her conferences. Notice that she uses her observations from this lesson to predict a misconception she might see the following day about how to write three-digit numbers. She then plans to use a recording sheet that will support students in thinking about the ways to write three-digit numbers to match what they stand for conceptually.

Anticipating Students' Struggles and Strategies

Each of the previous ways to respond to student thinking supports you in crafting immediate instruction, today or tomorrow. Perhaps the most fruitful response to conferring over the long term is to use what you notice today to help you anticipate what students might do in the future. Although this has real benefits for immediate instruction, anticipation has a more robust impact—it builds your understanding of the common struggles and the ways student thinking develops within each of the concepts taught in your grade level, what is referred to as *pedagogical content knowledge*. Pedagogical content knowledge can help you to anticipate misconceptions, build mental maps of how students often learn over time, pace instruction, and plan tasks that support conceptual learning. As you confer with students around tasks tied to a mathematical concept, you are getting windows into how children learn about these ideas, which will help you with all students—those in front of you now and those to come in the years ahead.

Guiding Questions for Anticipating Struggles and Strategies in the Future

Listening to students talk about their thinking, consider what it teaches you about a concept by reflecting on the following questions:

- What makes learning this idea challenging for students?
- Where do students get stuck? What gets them unstuck?
- How do their strategies evolve?
- What understandings are they drawing on to make sense?
- What mathematical connections do they make or find useful?

To reflect on what you might anticipate for the coming days, consider the following questions:

- What strategies were used across the class? How common were they?
- What did students struggle with today? What does that tell me about what they understand and don't yet understand?

Getting Ready to Respond Through Anticipation

Each conference is an opportunity to add to your mental map of how students learn and think about mathematical concepts. As your map becomes richer, it will be easier to anticipate places students might get stuck, what connections you could support them in making, or how you might nudge their strategies in ways that make developmental sense. You may want to actually create concept maps for yourself tied to each unit of instruction where you web the big ideas involved in, say, your measurement unit, the common struggles, the ways strategies progress, observations of the ways representations change, and useful questions you asked during conferring to support student thinking. Knowing that it may be a year before you revisit these ideas with students again, recording what you notice about each concept or group of concepts through conferring can help you build a powerful resource that can inform your planning in the future.

Beyond building a network of student thinking, you will want to consider what strategies and struggles you could anticipate being part of your classroom in the coming days. For instance, if one group struggled with tens and ones during a task on subtraction today, then it makes sense that this same struggle could be present tomorrow for the same or other groups. By studying what helped this group move through their struggle, you can build a toolkit of possible moves you could use if you saw this struggle emerge tomorrow with a different group. Similarly, you will likely see multiple strategies for any given task. If you support one group in beginning to use place value to solve a problem, it can help you learn the cues that students are ready to make this move—an insight that can help you anticipate how you might confer with other students in the coming days. Your class as a whole is a glimpse at a continuum of learning. By seeing that some of your students are starting to use place value, say, you know that others will soon be ready for this shift, too. You can begin to locate your class on the map you've been constructing, which gives you a sense of where students might go tomorrow.

> ### USING CONFERRING TO ANTICIPATE STUDENT THINKING
>
> Faith reflects on what she noticed from her conferring during a task in which students were asked: "If I have 20 packs of 10 pencils and 4 loose ones, how many pencils do I have?" The data she gathered across her class help Faith map what makes the concept of place value challenging when students extend their thinking from two-digit numbers to three-digit numbers and the strategies that students could use to build their understanding of why this quantity is represented as 204 rather than 24. This is an example of using conferring to build pedagogical content knowledge around place value that can support Faith in her work with these students and future second graders.

Keeping Records

Keeping records of your conferring can help you to respond to what you've learned and track how learning unfolds over time. These records can support you in making the instructional decisions we've already discussed in this chapter, and they can facilitate communicating about student learning to others, in parent conferences, with special educators, or among coteachers. As you are learning to confer, keeping records may seem daunting, but once you begin to feel comfortable with eliciting and nudging student thinking, you'll want to think about how to track progress and trends.

Your record-keeping structure needs to include at least two features. First, you'll want to track the dates on which you conferred with each student, so that you can be aware of how long it has been since you saw a student's thinking in action. Second, you'll want a way to make notes about what happened in the conference that you'd like to remember. For instance, in a unit about developing strategies for multiplication, you'd want to make note of the particular strategy each student or group was trying so you can see how they evolve during the unit. Other aspects of students' work may also be worth noting; for instance, if the students in the group were struggling to collaborate, you'd want to see if this was a persistent issue. Notes need not be long descriptions; they can be short reminders of the important features you noticed, such as "Challenges working together. Sarah taking over. Nudged collaboration," or, "Used Unifix cubes to count one by one. Working on counting with accuracy."

There are a few other issues to consider when deciding how to organize your notes. First, do you want to take notes on individual students or the groups of collaborating students? If your students are consistently, over some period of time, working with the same partners, it may be simpler to organize your notes by group. If partners rotate regularly or students are frequently absent and groups need to be flexible, then you may want to organize your notes by student. Finally, it's useful to include space to jot ideas for how to respond to the data you've gathered. If there are particularly useful reflection questions, you might want them handy to help prompt your thinking as you take notes or look over them after the lesson.

You can make your own record-keeping structure, whether in a notebook or a form you can photocopy for each week or two of conferring. In the appendix, I have included a few sample note-taking templates to help you think about what might work best for you. The templates are also available to download at http://hein.pub/IntheMoment-login (see page vii or 129 for login info). If you have other ways of taking anecdotal records that work well for you during other parts of your teaching day, I encourage you to think about simply adapting those for conferring in math.

HOW CONFERRING FITS IN

6.5 Mary reflects on how conferring holds her mathematics instruction together, and how she makes time to confer. Mary talks about the kinds of records she keeps and how she uses these day to day and across a unit of instruction.

COMMON QUESTIONS

What about all the kids I didn't talk to today?

You are not going to be able to talk to every child or group every day. Keeping records of your conferring will help you to know how long it has been since the last time you conferred with a particular student or group so that you can gather consistent data on how the student's or group's learning is progressing. Each day you'll need to make decisions about which groups you'd like to confer with, and those decisions are likely to be informed by the conferences you had the previous day and your quick assessment of what is happening during today's work time. For instance, if you see a group visibly frustrated, you'll want to confer with these students regardless of how long it has been since you did so. You may want to talk to a group you conferred with the previous day to see how those students' thinking is developing or to revisit a conceptual struggle. And you'll want to be mindful of groups you didn't have time to talk to yesterday.

In balancing all of these needs, you should find yourself getting a solid sample of your class each day. The groups you talk to won't tell you everything that is happening, but they should give you a sense of the conceptual landscape your students are in, how the class is progressing, and what the struggles are. These data will allow you to shape the closing discussion and the task for the next day, each of which offer new opportunities to gather additional data by hearing more voices. And tomorrow you get another chance to confer.

What if there don't seem to be trends? Or if my kids are in many different places?

Sometimes you will select a task that you believe will support students in thinking about a mathematical concept and as you confer you learn that each group is grappling with very different challenges—or no challenge at all. For instance, you might confer with four groups to find one struggling to collaborate, one operating under a misconception around the central mathematical concept, another solving the problem with confidence and working on representations to share, and a final group so confused and frustrated they don't know where to begin. Such a scenario is entirely possible and offers no clear trend.

As surprising as it may seem, this likely indicates that you have selected an appropriately challenging task, and that your conferring is supporting students in the many different places that they are learning. This is the central strength of conferring—it is a tool for differentiated instruction. When your students appear to be in many places, conferring is a venue for speaking to each group about their understandings and how they are evolving.

However, you are still left with decisions about how to shape the closing discussion and the next day's task. The discussion can do one of two things. It can either serve as a place for the class to come together to make sense out of the task, even if you do not discuss the answer(s), or it can be a setting for sharing what's possible by showcasing a solution pathway that one group developed. You will need to decide which makes the most sense given the data you have collected. If your data indicate a vast spread in the ways students are engaging with the task, on the following day they might need a similar task that gives them another chance to try out their thinking. If you do plan a similar task, then today's discussion is preparation for this second opportunity. Consider what will give students the best traction when they sit down the following day.

REFLECTING ON YOUR OWN PRACTICE

As you think about the assessment data you gather when conferring, the following guiding questions might help you reflect on your practice:

- When do you reflect on the data you have gathered during conferring? How can you build in time for this reflection in your daily routines?
- How do you already use conferring data as formative assessment? What goals will you set for using conferring data to inform instruction?
- What kinds of reflection questions do you want to ask yourself during and after conferring? What new reflective habits would you like to build?
- What kinds of informal records do you keep in other parts of your teaching that work for you? How might you adapt these to keep records of conferring in math?
- What kinds of records do you keep of your daily plans? How can you use them to record what you learned about student thinking, the discussion questions you posed, or what you plan for the next day?
- How could conferring data help you communicate student learning with parents or co-teachers?

7

Learning to Confer

How can you learn to confer? Once you've gotten started, how can you grow your conferring practice? Learning to confer involves learning to navigate all the parts of a conference, from uncovering student thinking to building an interpretation and navigating a nudge. But every interaction is different, and it requires a great deal of practice and reflection to become comfortable improvising your way from entering a conference to closing with a nudge. How can you get practice and grow?

So far in this book, we've looked at how a conference builds, starting from the first eliciting question. Because each move you take depends on what has come before, learning to confer follows the same journey as a conference itself.

First, teachers learn to elicit student thinking. Along the way, they must learn to interpret the work students are doing through the answers they provide, the manipulatives they use, and what they have recorded. It makes sense to spend time just focusing on this part of the process, without the pressure to nudge student thinking yet. This also gives your *students* a chance to learn to confer, as they learn to answer your questions and gain practice and confidence in explaining their ideas. If students have never been asked to justify, probing questions can seem like an interrogation and student confidence can crumble. They may need explicit messages about the value you place on their thinking, lots of encouragement, and sufficient time to build the capacity to make their thinking visible. There is strong evidence that giving students the opportunity to explain their thinking and justify why it makes sense, even as that thinking develops, supports conceptual learning (Franke et al. 2009; Webb et al. 2009).

After you and students both feel confident in your capacity to uncover students' thinking and make sense out of the reasoning behind it, it is time to study nudging. Learning to nudge is, again, a partnership with students. It involves making a decision about the pathway for nudging: conceptual understanding, developing a strategy, representation, communication, or collaboration. Then you need to decide on a move to initiate the nudge and coordinate moves to help students construct some new understanding or pathway forward in their work. In navigating, you must attend to what students say back to you and make adaptations to respond to what seems to be working and any signals that students are pushing back (see Chapter 5).

Later in this chapter, we'll look at how to navigate this learning using different activities and partnerships, keeping in mind that *what* you focus on learning will need to evolve over time. Also in this chapter, we'll examine activities that provide opportunities for practice, as well as ways you can work both with your colleagues and independently, in partnership with your students, to develop your conferring practice. First, we'll look at three structures you can use. Then, we'll think about who you might partner with in your learning. These sections are designed to provide choices that you can mix and match to create an evolving experience for your own learning. No one activity is enough, and you may shift among different kinds of partnerships along the way. You may, for instance, find that you benefit from different structures as you learn to elicit and interpret student thinking than when you work on nudging. As you try out different ways of learning, reflect on how the structures are working for you and what you need to grow.

It is also worth noting that students need to learn to confer, too. As teachers learn to surface their thinking by asking effective eliciting and probing questions, students are learning how to answer these questions. Before you launch into conferring with students, consider what skills they already have at explaining their thinking and how they might respond emotionally. This is yet another reason to devote energy first to eliciting, probing, and interpreting student thinking. ■

Structures for Learning to Confer

In this section, we'll examine three structures you can use to learn as you build your skill in eliciting, probing, interpreting, and nudging, as well as handling challenges that emerge along the way. First, video provides a safe space to examine student thinking and teacher moves without the pressure to respond quickly, and at the end of this chapter you'll find a bank of videos from Mary and Faith's classrooms to use for immediate practice. Second, video can also be used to capture, revisit, and reflect on your own practice, allowing you to consider what happened when you have more time to think and set goals. Finally, working with students in the classroom reintroduces the demand to think quickly and respond in the moment, a major source of challenge when conferring.

As you make choices, consider the skills you and your students already have and how you can bring them into conferring. For instance, if students already explain their thinking during number talks (Humphreys and Parker 2015; Parrish 2014) and you have experience interpreting their thinking on your feet, then you all may be ready to dive into eliciting questions and conferring with a colleague. However, if this is more unfamiliar territory, starting with the video provided at the end of this chapter may make more sense. Let's look at each activity in turn, what it has to offer, and how to try it out.

Looking at Video from This Book

At the end of this chapter you'll find a bank of videos you can use to support your learning. Looking at video taken in an unknown classroom gives you some distance from the immediacy of teaching and reduces the stakes of the decisions you make. You do not need to be fast or right. Video is simply a place to try. But try what? These videos can be used for four different purposes: studying eliciting, practicing interpreting student thinking, practicing making decisions about nudging, and studying nudging.

Studying Eliciting

Watch the videos in the eliciting section of the resources or the first parts of the videos on making nudging decisions to examine how the teacher navigates eliciting. What moves does she use? When and how does she press for reasoning? How does she make thinking public? How does she navigate the partnership when eliciting? When does she stop? Why? These videos are exhibits of real, live conferring as it happened in classrooms, so the ways teachers elicited varied. What do you notice about the variation in eliciting? Why is one video different from another, and what does that tell you about what might be possible in your classroom? You can use these videos for this kind of close study of interaction to help you get ready to confer with your own students.

Practicing Interpreting Student Thinking

Watch the videos in the eliciting section of the resources or the first parts of the videos on making decisions and at the end, pause to practice interpreting the student thinking that emerged from the teacher's moves. How do you understand what students were thinking? What do you think they understand, don't yet understand, or misunderstand? What are they trying? Try to construct a complete interpretation of the students' thinking based on the evidence you can see and hear. Take advantage of the nature of video to rewind and watch the whole interaction or specific parts repeatedly. Be sure to tie your conjectures back to the evidence in the video. If more than one interpretation is possible, what could students be thinking? Why? By starting with this slow, deliberate form of interpreting, you can use these videos to prepare for interpreting student thinking on your feet.

Practicing Making Decisions About Nudging

Watch videos in the eliciting section of the resources or the first parts of the videos on making decisions and at the end, pause to practice making decisions about what type of nudge you think students need and what you might say to initiate that nudge. What type of nudge do you think these students could benefit from now? What is your evidence? Why not a different type of nudge? How is this type of nudge connected to the thinking that was elicited? Take advantage of the opportunity to debate this decision, and think carefully about connecting the type of nudge to what students revealed. Then brainstorm some questions you could ask to point students down this pathway. What might you ask to open the door to thinking about concepts, strategies, representations, communication, or collaboration? What moves would you anticipate needing to support this nudge? Why? What would you do if students pushed back or gave you a blank stare? You can use this practice making careful decisions to prepare for making these same decisions in real time with your own students.

Studying Nudging

Watch the videos in the section on making decisions to examine how the teacher and students work together to construct a nudge. It makes sense to do this step after you have had a chance to engage in the other ways of using the video described previously, including planning how you might nudge these students. You can then watch how these teachers nudged their students and compare what they did to your own plan. Knowing that you cannot fully plan a nudge because you must respond to what students say, the nudge in the video will likely diverge from your plan. What decisions did the teacher make? How did the teacher shape the nudge in response to what students said? What moves did she use? Why did those moves make sense in that moment? What else could the teacher have said? What surprised you about the way the nudge unfolded? How did the teacher maintain students' ownership over their work? How can you tell that the students' thinking has been advanced? What evidence did you see or hear? You can use these videos for this kind of close study of nudging to help you prepare to nudge your own students' thinking.

Looking at Your Own Video

You (or a colleague) may be ready to try conferring with your own students. Making video or audio records of your conferences can create a useful tool for reflection, discussion, and growth. You can use a smartphone, an audio recorder, or a camera to capture the conferences you try on a given day and then return later to review the data you collected. You can watch or listen on your own or with partners. A private viewing can sometimes feel more comfortable, while watching with colleagues creates the opportunity for discussion. (We'll talk more about this on page 119.) As you watch, you can use the videos to revisit the decisions and interpretations you formed and consider other moves you could have tried. The questions below provide some framework for reflection:

- What do you notice about what students are doing and saying?
- What do they understand? Not yet understand? Misunderstand?
- What is your evidence for your interpretation?
- What moves did you use to uncover student thinking?
- How did you probe for reasoning?
- What else could you have asked to clarify what students did, thought, or meant?
- What other probing questions could have been useful, if any?
- What decision did you make about the type of nudge students needed? Why?
- How did you try to nudge? What moves did you use? How did you respond to what students offered back?
- Did you encounter any challenges? If so, what? Why? How did you respond?

- What moves could you have used to support nudging or address challenges?
- What can you learn from this conference about the students? About conferring?
- What are you wondering now?

You certainly do not need to tackle all of these questions. Instead, choose some questions that focus on the areas of conferring you are working on and spend some time reflecting on what happened and what it can teach you about your practice. Based on what you see when you have more time to study your teaching and your students, consider setting some clear, compact goals, such as giving more wait time or asking more probing questions.

If you are viewing video with colleagues, keep in mind that you can learn from watching video of their conferring, too. You and your partners need norms for watching and discussing video together to keep this a safe activity, rather than one that leads to vulnerability. Be sure to discuss ahead of viewing the need to stay grounded in the evidence, remain free of judgment, be curious about student thinking and practice, and think aloud constructively to support future conferring. Some useful stems for discussion can be, "I notice . . . ," "I wonder . . . ," and "What if . . . ?"

Who You Can Learn With: Working Alone or Together

Learning is fundamentally social. People must interact to learn, which is why collaborative problem-solving and conferring are important structures for the mathematics classroom. Consider yourself as a learner and how you can structure social interactions to support your own learning of conferring. You can work with children; they are your partners in conferring and you can approach your practice in the classroom as an opportunity to learn from students. You can also work with colleagues, either one-on-one or in larger teams, to generate supportive collegial conversation about student thinking and the pedagogies involved in conferring. Each school community has different collegial resources, and you may find partners for learning in unexpected places, including other grade levels, with special educators, student teachers, math specialists, and coaches. Cast your net wide to find folks to talk to and work with as you learn to confer.

In the following sections, we'll examine how and what you can learn from three different social arrangements: independent learning, learning with a coach or colleague, and learning with a team. Each of these structures offers particular opportunities for learning. We'll examine what activities match best to each kind of social structure and ways that you might take advantage of what each has to offer your learning.

Learning on Your Own

No matter what colleagues are available to partner with you, your students are there to learn with and from you. The major advantage to working on your own is that you do not need to muster collegial resources, find time to meet, or negotiate the goals. You can devote as much attention as you want for as long as you want to learn what you want. The major challenge with learning alone is the absence of other voices that can add to your thinking, notice something different in students' work, construct an alternate interpretation, or brainstorm moves.

Tools for Working Independently

Learning to confer independently involves what you are doing now— reading—and identifying some ways to practice and try out your ideas in your classroom. The most effective ways to learn on your own include the following:

- Use the guiding questions at the end of each chapter in this book to support reflection on your practice.
- Watch videos of conferring, like those at the end of the chapter, and ask questions to support your own inquiry and study.
- Confer with your own students.
  - ▶ Take notes about the moves you found most effective to build your practice.
  - ▶ Take notes about student thinking to practice using the data as formative assessment.
  - ▶ Video- or audio-record the interactions and listen to them after school to reflect on your own moves, notice trends in your practice, and set goals.
  - ▶ Ask your students to reflect on how conferring is going and what is helping them to learn.

Learning with a Coach or Colleague

Partnering with a colleague or coach can amplify what you learn by adding opportunities to talk about practice in detail and tied to specific situations.

Partnering with a math or instructional coach, if you have one in your school, can be particularly productive because they do not have their own classroom and can enter yours without the need for coverage. You can also partner with a teaching colleague, whether it's someone who teaches on your grade-level team, provides inclusion support in your classroom, or is just an interested teacher at another grade. Collegial conversation adds new ways of thinking about instructional situations and sparks deeper, more critical reflection. The most significant challenges to partnering with a colleague are identifying someone who shares your interest in learning to confer and with whom you feel comfortable being vulnerable about your practice. Time is also an issue but can be easier to find with just one colleague than with a team.

Conferring Together

As we've seen, there is a lot you can learn from conferring in your own classroom and reflecting afterward, with or without video. However, you can get a lot more power out of learning through conferring if you confer side by side with a colleague. This notion breaks many norms that we have around teaching as a private or personal act and instead turns teaching into a collaborative activity. Conferring with a colleague means circulating around the room together, conferring with students together, and solving the problems that emerge in the moment together (Figure 7.1). The big benefit to conferring together is the opportunity to talk about what you are noticing and the decisions you make as they happen. You can brainstorm questions to ask, get ideas about how to interpret student thinking, or sort through confusions when you still have time to act on your ideas. You can learn about conferring while you are supporting student learning.

There are several ways to collaborate with a colleague while conferring side by side. It can help to talk ahead of time about which of these structures you want to try or which feel most supportive of the learning you're aiming for. That said, I encourage you to move between

FIGURE 7.1 Mary and me conferring together with a pair of students

these structures, rather than sticking rigidly to any one. When you confer with another adult by your side, you can try the following:

LEAD CONFERRING AND REFLECT TOGETHER. Sometimes it is useful to confer with your students as you would independently, but with a colleague next to you, listening and watching. Rarely in teaching do we have another adult witnessing the same things we do, which makes reflecting with a colleague challenging. By having a partner observe your conferring, you can step back after the interaction and talk as you walk to the next conference about what happened, what they noticed, what you both learned, and what that might mean for the next interaction. These brief reflections before you dive into the next interaction can fuel trying something different straightaway or developing hunches about student thinking as you go.

ASK YOUR PARTNER TO LEAD CONFERRING, OBSERVE, AND REFLECT TOGETHER. Alternatively, you may want to observe a colleague interacting with your students. This creates a rare opportunity to observe your students and practice in the moment without being responsible for making the decisions. You might see something in their work that you wouldn't have otherwise, or you might notice something about your colleague's conferring practice that you want to try yourself. Again, reflect on what you observe after the interaction is closed, as you walk to the next conference. One useful way to use this and the previous structure is to alternate who leads and who observes.

COFACILITATE CONFERRING. You and a partner can each have a voice in a conference, offering questions or moves when they seem appropriate. Some teams find that when one teacher begins the interaction, they get to a point where they want their colleague to step in with a move. Coparticipation in conferring can give you both the opportunity to shape the direction of the conference and each other's learning about practice at the same time. However you both navigate the interaction, reflecting together as you walk to the next conference can help you think about what you are learning from each other and what you want to try next.

PAUSE THE INTERACTION TO MAKE DECISIONS TOGETHER. Sometimes you may be conferring and get stuck. Perhaps you are really confused about what the students are thinking, and your questions haven't helped you gain any clarity. Perhaps you know precisely what students are thinking but are unsure what to do next to nudge. Perhaps students have posed a question or offered information that you haven't encountered before, and you have no experience to draw on.

Whatever the reason for feeling stuck, if you are conferring side by side with a colleague, you can pause the interaction to talk through this challenge in the moment. Although this might sound disruptive or difficult to manage, students are typically very cooperative when these pauses are brief. In my own experience, it often only takes one minute to step back a foot or two with a colleague and make sense of what students are doing or decide on the next move to make. Ask you partner the question that is your obstacle: "What do you think they are doing?" "What should I say next?" "What kind of nudge do you think they need?" Talk it over briefly and then dive back in. These pauses can be powerful moments for learning about practice because you can act immediately on your ideas, test them out, and see what happens.

Gaining comfort conferring together can take some time. Being a partner in the moment means thinking about student learning, your practice, and adult learning simultaneously. Just as colleagues need norms for viewing video together, they need norms for collaborating around practice in the moment. Consider developing some signals for when you want your partner's help or when you want them to step back. Furthermore, colleagues need ways of capturing what they are learning, such as reflecting together after the lesson or taking notes on productive moves as you work together. At the end of each lesson, consider reflecting briefly on some of the following questions:

- What did you notice today?
- What did you learn about conferring?
- What moves were productive? How do you know? (Write these down!)
- What helped you to elicit student thinking?
- What challenges did you face in interpreting student thinking? What did you do that was useful?
- Which conferences felt really good? Why? What did you do?
- How did you nudge today? What did you do to make that nudge happen?
- What are your students learning about how to confer with you? How did you see that?
- What do you want to work on next in your conferring practice? What structures will be helpful?

Tools for Working Together

Learning to confer with a colleague or coach could include any of the activities that you can do alone, the side-by-side conferring described previously, and partnering in any of the following ways:

- Watch videos of conferring, like those at the end of the chapter, and discuss what you notice using the activities described earlier. Brainstorm about what these videos can teach you about practice.
- Confer independently in your own classroom.
  - ▶ Video- or audio-record your conferences to watch together and discuss. If your partner has his own classroom, you can watch each other's videos together.
  - ▶ Take notes as you confer and reflect with your partner at the end of the day about what you noticed, what you're wondering, and what you want to try next.

Learning with a Team

Working in a team can open up discussion to many different voices, experiences, and ideas. Schools use a variety of team learning structures, such as professional learning communities, grade-level teams, coaching groups, or book study groups. Positioning learning to confer within one of these existing collaborative structures can mean that time is already devoted to learning and it can feel more like teacher-driven professional development. These groups often offer some soft accountability to try new things, bring video to share, or reflect on your practice with some regularity.

Tools for Working in a Group

Learning to confer with a group of colleagues could include any of the activities that you can do alone or with a partner, as well as taking advantage of the power of a team in any of the following ways:

- Engage in a book study, discussing the ideas that emerge and the guiding questions for reflection at the end of each chapter.
- Watch videos of conferring, like those at the end of this chapter, and use the activities described earlier to fuel group discussion.
- Conferring independently in your own classroom.
  - ▶ Video- or audio-record your conferences to watch together and discuss. Each person in the group should have opportunities to bring video for discussion. You can discuss several videos in one meeting or rotate who is responsible for bringing videos for the group to learn from.
  - ▶ Reflect as a group on how conferring is going in each person's classroom, offering ideas, and setting goals.
  - ▶ Take notes after conferring to bring to the group examples of effective moves or questions you want to get input on from the group.

- Confer side by side by breaking into pairs within your larger group so that each person has a colleague who can come into their classroom, and each person gets the opportunity to try conferring in another classroom, too.

Resources for Learning

The videos in this section are intended as places to practice interpreting student thinking and considering the decisions that are made during conferring. There are two types of videos provided. The first section includes videos of only the first portion of conferring, when the teacher elicits and probes student thinking. The second section includes full conferences, from eliciting to nudging.

Videos to Practice Eliciting, Noticing, and Interpreting Student Thinking

Use these videos to study eliciting and to practice noticing and interpreting student thinking. Consider what you might do next when conferring with these students. All of the following clips come from Mary's fourth-grade class on days when students were working to make sense of the traditional algorithm for subtraction, which they had all learned in previous grades.

PRACTICE: ELICITING, NOTICING, AND INTERPRETING

 On this day Mary presented her students with the following task:

The factory has an inventory of 381 small T-shirts. A customer bought 129 small T-shirts. How many small T-shirts are there now?

She then showed them some work based on a common misconception in her class about how to model subtraction using base ten blocks. She showed how a fictitious student the class named Alex had represented 381 T-shirts with base ten blocks. The student had crossed out 1 hundred block and 2 tens rods. Then, seeing he didn't have enough ones left to cross out 9 ones, he added 9 ones instead. Mary asked the class to determine whether or not Alex's work was correct and come up with a justification for their answer. Watch the clip to see Mary elicit thinking from two students who partnered on this task.

PRACTICE: ELICITING, NOTICING, AND INTERPRETING

The following two clips both took place the next day, when Mary again offered students work from a fictitious student, whom the class named Jeffy, and asked them to determine if and why it made sense. Jeffy had been solving a problem that involved starting with 1,707 T-shirts, then selling 550 of those shirts. When he subtracted using the traditional algorithm, he found that there were 1,257 T-shirts remaining. In this work Jeffy has made an error the students often make, simply subtracting the smaller digit from the larger one without attending to the meaning of what they are doing.

 Mary and I conferred with two students on the carpet soon after the class started working on the task. Watch the clip to see the thinking elicited and how we navigate some blank stares.

 Mary conferred with this pair of students who quickly name that they are stuck. Watch the clip to see how Mary elicits thinking to better understand where these students are.

Videos to Practice Making Decisions to Nudge

These videos are intended to support you in learning to make decisions about how to nudge student thinking in the moment. Each video is segmented into the part of the conference in which the teacher elicits and probes student thinking and a second part in which the teacher nudges. Between these two parts of the video there is a blank screen so you can pause to reflect on the elicited student thinking and think about how you might nudge these students, before seeing what the teacher did. All of the following clips come from Faith's second-grade class on days when they were working on place value by counting collections of objects or solving problems involving collections.

PRACTICE: MAKING DECISIONS TO NUDGE

 In this clip Faith sits down with two students counting pattern blocks on the carpet. The class has learned to make groups of 10 to make counting easier. Notice how Faith is observing surfacing student thinking as students work in this clip.

PRACTICE: MAKING DECISIONS TO NUDGE

7.5

7.6

The following two clips come from the same day, on which Faith presented students with the following task:

> **My mom bought a bunch of Halloween pencils. She bought 20 packs of 10 pencils and 4 loose ones. How many Halloween pencils did my mom buy?**

Faith wanted students to grapple with numbers in the hundreds while still thinking with groups of 10. Watch these clips to see how Faith elicits students' thinking about this task and nudges that thinking forward when the partnerships have different ideas at the start of each conference.

COMMON QUESTIONS

Where do I get started?

The most straightforward and lowest-risk place to begin is by watching and analyzing the videos in this chapter, or even returning to videos in previous chapters to do the same work. It can be useful to see several videos back-to-back and make comparisons across them. How did the teacher elicit differently in these two cases? Why? What made the nudges different? You can use the videos to collect moves you'd like to try with your own students. I encourage you to focus first on eliciting and interpreting student thinking. If you can recruit a learning partner to elicit and interpret with you, having conversations in the moment about student thinking gives you the opportunity to make adjustments, test theories, and ask additional questions—all of which sharpen your own learning while supporting your students. These are the most effective places to begin learning to confer.

I feel like my learning is progressing slowly. What can I do?

To boost your own learning you need the voices of others and time to reflect analytically. Two useful ways to introduce these into your practice are by conferring with a partner in your own classroom or by inviting others to watch and discuss video of you conferring. Both venues create spaces for colleagues to offer you new ideas, moves, or interpretations and to ask you questions that spur your thinking. If you haven't yet tried these activities, I recommend that you recruit at least one colleague who could support your thinking, and hopefully this person could engage in their own learning as well.

I often get stuck in conferring with the same kids again and again. How can I learn to nudge them?

Some students are easier to confer with than others, simply because they are more proficient in articulating their thinking and making it visible. Others may be more challenging because they are quieter, more reticent to offer their thinking, or struggle to put their ideas into words. These same students may also be among those who have not experienced success in mathematics in the past. These students deserve our attention and will get meaningful benefits from every opportunity to communicate and reflect on their own thinking. They may have ways of communicating that you need to learn how to interpret. The better you get at interpreting their thinking, the more willing they may be to take risks in offering it.

This is an analytic task—figuring out what these students are saying and what they need—that is best accomplished with several minds and a reservoir of time not available in the classroom. I encourage you to video-record several attempts to confer with the students you often struggle to nudge and then watch this video with colleagues with the express goal of gaining insight into these students. Invite colleagues to offer you multiple possible interpretations of these students' thinking—what *could* they mean? Mine your teaching partners for moves you could try to get yourself and the conference unstuck. Take these many theories and ideas back to your classroom to test them out. You will learn more about these students with every new attempt, and you can return to your colleagues with new data to try again if needed.

REFLECTING ON YOUR OWN PRACTICE

As you plan for and try learning to confer, the following guiding questions might help you reflect on your learning:

- What activities for learning feel like a good match for you and what you hope to learn?
- What colleagues might be interested and supportive partners in your learning? How might you engage them?
- What resources in your school or professional community are available to support you in learning to confer? How could you use these?

- How might you use the videos in this chapter?
- After trying some learning activities, which feel the most supportive of your learning? Why?
- How could you string different learning structures together to make a complete system to support your learning?

Closing Thoughts

Talking to kids and watching them learn is the best part of teaching. As you head into your classroom to launch your conferring practice, remember to be curious about all that your students can do and are doing right now. Every child makes sense—your job is to find the sense and build on it. This is not a simple task, but it is worthy of your efforts and your struggle. Remember that the learning we do with children as we teach can be the most fruitful, enduring, and taxing professional development we engage in. Listen hard. Give yourself—and your students—the grace to learn how to talk to one another about complex ideas. And celebrate. Celebrate when a question gets an unexpected answer, or an answer at all. Celebrate when you suddenly see the math through the eyes of your students. Celebrate when you learn something new about a child. Celebrate when you and your students feel that nudge forward. And stay curious.

Appendix:
Sample Conferring Notes Templates

 Scan this QR code or visit http://hein.pub/ IntheMoment-login to access printable, full page versions of the appendixes. (Enter your email address and password or click "Create a New Account." Once you have logged in, enter key code **ITMOM** and click "Register.")

Dates: _____ Conceptual Focus: _____

Partners: _____	Partners: _____	Partners: _____
Partners: _____	Partners: _____	Partners: _____
Partners: _____	Partners: _____	Partners: _____
Partners: _____	Partners: _____	Partners: _____

Instructional Ideas:
Discussion questions, tasks, or conferring priorities you'd like to remember.

Dates: _____ Conceptual Focus: _____

Group: _____ Date Notes	Group: _____ Date Notes
Group: _____ Date Notes	Group: _____ Date Notes
Group: _____ Date Notes	Group: _____ Date Notes
Group: _____ Date Notes	Group: _____ Date Notes

Instructional Ideas:
Discussion questions, tasks, or conferring priorities you'd like to remember.

Dates: _____ Conceptual Focus: _____

Student: _____	Student: _____	Student: _____	Student: _____
Date Notes	Date Notes	Date Notes	Date Notes
Student: _____	Student: _____	Student: _____	Student: _____
Date Notes	Date Notes	Date Notes	Date Notes
Student: _____	Student: _____	Student: _____	Student: _____
Date Notes	Date Notes	Date Notes	Date Notes
Student: _____	Student: _____	Student: _____	Student: _____
Date Notes	Date Notes	Date Notes	Date Notes
Student: _____	Student: _____	Student: _____	Student: _____
Date Notes	Date Notes	Date Notes	Date Notes
Student: _____	Student: _____	Student: _____	Student: _____
Date Notes	Date Notes	Date Notes	Date Notes

Instructional Ideas:
Discussion questions, tasks, or conferring priorities you'd like to remember.

Appendix: Sample Conferring Notes Templates

Dates: _____ Conceptual Focus: _____

Group or Partners	M	T	W	Th	F

Instructional Ideas:
Discussion questions, tasks, or conferring priorities you'd like to remember.

Bibliography

Anderson C. 2000. *How's It Going?* Portsmouth, NH: Heinemann.

Black P., and D. Wiliam. 1998. "Assessment and Classroom Learning." *Assessment in Education: Principles, Policy & Practice* 5 (1): 7–74. http://doi.org/10.1080/0969595980050102.

Calkins, L. M. 1986. *The Art of Teaching Writing.* Portsmouth, NH: Heinemann.

———. 2001. *The Art of Teaching Reading.* New York: Longman.

Carter, S. 2008. "Disequilibrium & Questioning in the Primary Classroom: Establishing Routines That Help Students Learn." *Teaching Children Mathematics* 15 (3): 134–137.

Chapin, S. H., M. C. O'Connor, and N.C. Anderson. 2013. *Classroom Discussions in Math: A Teacher's Guide for Using Talk Moves to Support the Common Core and More.* 3rd ed. Saulsalito, CA: Math Solutions.

Cohen, E. G., and R. A. Lotan. 2014. *Designing Groupwork: Strategies for the Heterogeneous Classroom.* 3rd ed. New York: Teachers College Press.

Common Core State Standards Initiative. 2010. *Common Core State Standards for Mathematics.* Washington, D.C.

Duckworth, E. 2006. *"The Having of Wonderful Ideas" and Other Essays on Teaching and Learning.* New York: Teachers College Press.

Engle, R. A., D. P. Lam, X. S. Meyer, and S. E. Nix. 2012. "How Does Expansive Framing Promote Transfer? Several Proposed Explanations and a Research Agenda for Investigating Them." *Educational Psychologist* 47 (3): 215–31. http://doi.org/10.1080/00461520.2012.695678.

Featherstone, H., S. Crespo, L. M. Jilk, J. A. Oslund, A. N. Parks, and M. B. Wood. 2011. *Smarter Together! Collaboration and Equity in the Elementary Mathematics Classroom.* Reston, VA: National Council of the Teachers of Mathematics.

Fosnot, C. 2008. *Contexts for Learning Mathematics: The T-Shirt Factory*. Portsmouth, NH: Heinemann.

Franke, M. L., N. M. Webb, A. G. Chan, M. Ing, D. Freund, and D. Battey. 2009. "Teacher Questioning to Elicit Students' Mathematical Thinking in Elementary School Classrooms." *Journal of Teacher Education* 60 (4): 380–92.

Hiebert, J., T. Carpenter, E. Fennema, K. Fuson, D. Wearne, H. Murray, A. Olivier, and P. Human. 1997. *Making Sense: Teaching and Learning Mathematics with Understanding*. Portsmouth, NH: Heinemann.

Hiebert, J., and D. A. Grouws. 2007. "The Effects of Classroom Mathematics Teaching on Students' Learning." *Second Handbook of Research on Mathematics Teaching and Learning* 371–404.

Humphreys, C., and R. Parker. 2015. *Making Number Talks Matter: Developing Mathematical Practices and Deepening Understanding, Grades 4–10*. Portland, ME: Stenhouse.

Jacobs, V. R., L. L. C. Lamb, and R. A. Philipp. 2010. "Professional Noticing of Children's Mathematical Thinking." *Journal for Research in Mathematics Education* 41 (2): 169–202.

Kazemi, E., and D. Stipek. 2001. "Promoting Conceptual Thinking in Four Mathematics Classrooms." *The Elementary School Journal* 102 (1): 59–80.

Munson, J. 2016. "Improving the Productivity of Teacher-Student Interactions: A Consideration of Student Pushback and Ways to Respond." *New England Mathematics Journal* 49 (2): 16–25.

———. 2018. "Two Instructional Moves to Promote Student Competence." *Teaching Children Mathematics* 24 (4): 244–49.

National Council of the Teachers of Mathematics. 2014. *Principles to Actions: Ensuring Mathematical Success for All*. Reston, VA: National Council of Teachers of Mathematics.

Parrish, S. 2014. *Number Talks: Helping Children Build Mental Math and Computation Strategies*. Saulsalito, CA: Math Solutions.

Smith, M. S., and M. K. Stein. 2011. *5 Practices for Orchestrating Productive Mathematics Discussions*. Reston, VA: National Council of Teachers of Mathematics.

Teaching Works. 2014. "High-Leverage Practices." http://www.teachingworks.org/work-of-teaching/high-leverage-practices.

Vygotsky, L. S. 1978. *Mind in Society: The Development of Higher Psychological Processes*. Cambridge, MA: Harvard University Press.

Webb, N. M., M. L. Franke, T. De, A. G. Chan, D. Freund, P. Shein, and D. K. Melkonian. 2009. "'Explain to Your Partner': Teachers' Instructional

Practices and Students' Dialogue in Small Groups." *Cambridge Journal of Education* 39 (1): 49–70. http://doi.org/10.1080/03057640802701986.

Wood, T. (1998). Alternative Patterns of Communication in the Mathematics Classroom: Funneling or Focusing? In H. Steinbring, M. G. Bartolini-Bussi, & A. Sierpinska (Eds.), *Language and Communication in the Mathematics Classroom* (pp. 167–178). Reston, VA: National Council of the Teachers of Mathematics.

Further Reading

Rich Tasks

Boaler, J., J. Munson, and C. Williams. 2017. Mindset Mathematics series. San Francisco: Jossey-Bass.

Carpenter, T., E. Fennema, M. L. Franke, L. Levi, and S. B. Empson. 2014. *Children's Mathematics: Cognitively Guided Instruction.* 2nd ed. Portsmouth, NH: Heinemann.

Fosnot, C. 2008. Contexts for Learning Mathematics series. Portsmouth, NH: Heinemann.

Lilburn, P., and A. Ciurak. 2010. *Investigations, Tasks, and Rubrics to Teach and Assess Math, Grades 1–6.* Sausalito, CA: Math Solutions.

Small, M. 2009. *Good Questions: Great Ways to Differentiate Math Instruction.* New York: Teachers College Press.

Sullivan, P., and O. Lilburn. 2002. *Good Questions for Math Teaching: Why Ask Them and What to Ask, K–6.* Sausalito, CA: Math Solutions.

Facilitating Talk

Chapin, S. H., C. O'Connor, and N. C. Anderson. 2013. *Talk Moves: A Teacher's Guide for Using Classroom Discussions in Math, Grades K–6.* 3rd ed. Sausalito, CA: Math Solutions.

Smith, M.S., and M. K. Stein. 2011. *5 Practices for Orchestrating Productive Mathematics Discussions.* Reston, VA: National Council of Teachers of Mathematics.